LEE CANTER'S

HOMEWORK WITHOUT TEARS® FOR TEACHERS

Grades 7-12

A Publication of Lee Canter & Associates

Staff Writers
Marcia Shank
Jim Thompson

Illustrators
Tom Winberry
Bob McMahon
Gary Mouri

Cover Art
Patty Briles

Editorial Staff
Marlene Canter
Carol Provisor
Kathy Winberry

Design
Tom Winberry
Bob Winberry

ISBN #0-939007-33-9

Printed in the United States of America
First printing July 1989; Second printing April 1990

CONTENTS

PREFACE

To establish the best possible environment for teaching and learning in school, we at Lee Canter & Associates have developed a complete behavior management system— for teachers, administrators, support staff and parents. Our program, Assertive Discipline, has made a dramatic difference, nationwide, in the education of children.

In working with teachers over the years to solve behavior problems in school, we saw one issue surface again and again: problems with homework. Recently, Gallup Poll statistics showed that the most frequently recurring problem in school is the subject of homework.

To succeed in school, students must be able to do homework, and do it well. In our Homework Without Tears program, we're dedicated to helping them do that. In *Homework Without Tears for Teachers*, we'll show you your part in the homework process, and just how you can help your students achieve success.

Chapter 1
HOMEWORK WITHOUT TEARS

With homework, more is not necessarily better. As a matter of fact, unless homework is effective, we'd be better off without it. Homework that causes frustration and tears is much worse than no homework at all.

Lee Canter

If you are reading this, you care about making your homework assignments as effective as possible. And for good reason.

More teachers are assigning more homework in more grades than ever before. Many districts are adopting guidelines requiring teachers to give regular homework assignments. But why exactly is homework assigned? If you have never asked that question, you should.

You may believe, as many educators do, that homework can reinforce what you teach in the classroom, help to individualize your instruction, improve student performance, help students develop effective study habits and provide an important day-to-day link between home and school. Many researchers agree that effective homework can do all of this and more.

But have you ever thought of the negative impact homework can have when it is not effective?

If your students are frustrated because they can't do homework, they will end up in tears. If parents are upset because homework means nightly battles with their children, they may be in tears. And if you end up correcting mounds of papers that you feel are meaningless, then you may be in tears too.

Homework and You

Every time you give a homework assignment you are involving three groups of people in the homework process: your students, the parents and yourself. For homework to be effective, you must conscientiously give appropriate assignments, parents must provide support and motivation at home, and students must do the work themselves to the best of their ability.

When you think about it, homework asks for a lot from everyone involved. And you are the key. Homework starts and ends with you.

You are responsible for laying the groundwork for effective homework by:

- Teaching students how to schedule homework time, how to find an appropriate place in which to study, how to do the work themselves, and how to do their best work.

- Teaching students organizational skills that will help them develop responsible, independent work habits.

- Teaching students the study skills that will enable them to successfully pursue independent projects such as writing research reports and studying for tests.

- Communicating to parents when and how they should help their children, how to reinforce good work and how to deal with children who do not complete homework.

- Assigning work that your students can do, giving clear directions, collecting and checking assignments and providing consistent positive reinforcement to both students and parents.

Yes, this is going to take time and effort on your part. But if you give homework, it is going to take your (and parents' and students') time and effort one way or another. *Homework Without Tears for Teachers* will help you make the time and effort spent as profitable as possible by giving everyone involved the skills they need.

Homework and Parents

If there is a common cry among educators, it is a plea for more parental support. While homework has the potential of eliciting that support from parents, many times its misuse does exactly the opposite. Too often the parents' only first-hand experience with their children's education is a nightly confrontation over homework.

Homework can be, however, a golden opportunity to positively involve parents in the education of their children. One thing researchers do agree on is the importance of parents' interest and involvement to children's success in school. The more parents provide positive support, the better their children will achieve.

Homework is a daily opportunity for parents to help their children do better in school. Homework Without Tears will show you how to give parents the directions they need to be an important, positive part of their child's education.

Homework and Students in Grades 7-12

Often students who have had no problems with homework in the early grades suddenly find themselves trying desperately to keep their head above water when they reach middle school or high school. These students have difficulty with homework because they were not introduced to proper study skills in earlier grades. It is essential that you not assume that your students know how to select a study area, how to schedule homework time, or how to write down assignments. Keep in mind also that the skills that result in proper homework management—organizational skills, time management skills, etc., are the same skills students will soon be needing as they find employment.

The lessons in Chapter 5, "How to Teach Your Students to Do Homework Responsibly" will provide a solid base for homework assignments throughout the year.

You may also encounter students who for one reason or another simply refuse to do their homework. Chapter 8, "What to Do If Students Do Not Complete Homework," will give you techniques to get them back on the homework track.

What is Homework Without Tears?

Homework Without Tears is a systematic approach to effective homework based both on research and on the experience of master teachers. *Homework Without Tears for Teachers* will give you the ideas, materials and skills you need for yourself, your students and their parents to ensure homework is done consistently and responsibly.

This book will show you:

How to establish a homework policy.

- Guidelines for developing an effective homework policy and for communicating that policy to students and parents.

How to establish a Schoolwide Homework Plan.

- Guidelines for forming a Homework Coordinating Committee.

- Discussion of the responsibilities of the Homework Coordinating Committee.

How to involve parents in the homework process by giving them the skills they need to help their children succeed.

- A reproducible Homework Handbook for Parents that gives homework tips and study skills tips.

- Parent communication ideas designed to keep the lines of communication open between school and home.

How to teach your students to do homework.

- Nine lesson plans to teach students to do homework responsibly.

How to assign effective homework.

- Guidelines for determining effective homework assignments.

- Teacher-tested tips for collecting and correcting homework.

How to motivate students to do their homework.

- How to motivate individual students to do homework.

- Motivational techniques for your entire class.

What to do when students do not complete homework.

- Techniques you can use at school when students do not complete homework.

- Resource sheets for parents to use when their children do not do homework.

How to assign more creative homework.

- Creative Homework Models that can be applied to all subject areas.

Homework Without Tears for Teachers will make the homework process a more rewarding experience for you, your students and their parents. But the first step must be yours and there's no better time to start than right now.

Chapter 2
ESTABLISHING A HOMEWORK POLICY

Teachers who have an effective approach to homework start by developing a homework policy. The policy establishes a firm foundation for homework by stating your expectations for everyone involved in the homework process.

Your homework policy is important because it clearly spells out the type and amount of homework you will give, the manner in which you expect students to do their homework and the type and degree of support you expect from parents.

Many schools or districts already have a homework policy in place for you to use. If there is no such policy, it is important that you establish one on your own or with the help of your fellow teachers and your administrator.

Use the Homework Policy Planner (pages 93-94 of the Appendix) to help you determine your policy.

Follow these guidelines:

A homework policy should:

Give a rationale for homework.

You cannot assume that students or parents understand why homework is given or how important it is. Therefore, you should explain the benefits of homework and why you are going to give it. For instance, your rationale could include that homework is important because:

1. It reinforces skills and material learned in class.
2. It prepares students for upcoming class topics.
3. It teaches students to work independently.
4. It aids in evaluating student progress.
5. It teaches students to assume responsibility for their own work.
6. It teaches students organizational and time-management skills.

Explain the types of homework that will be assigned.

It is important that both parents and students know that you are doing your part to ensure that students have the ability to do the homework you assign.

Chapter 6, "5 Steps to Giving Effective Homework Assignments," will cover in detail the guidelines for assigning effective homework. Explain to parents and students the kinds of assignments they can expect in this class.

Inform parents and students of the amount and frequency of homework.

Research has shown that regular homework assignments produce more learning than less consistently assigned homework. It is important, therefore, for the homework policy to include:

- The days of the week on which you will assign homework.
- The amount of time it should take students to complete homework.

Provide guidelines for how students are to complete homework.

It is important for students to receive written instructions concerning how you expect homework assignments to be completed.
For example:

Guidelines for a math class
- All homework problems must be completed in pencil.
- Solutions must be shown.
- Answers only will not be accepted for credit.
- All homework must be completed on wide-lined 81/2" x 11" paper.
- Homework is expected to be completed on time. No credit is given for late, missing or incomplete assignments.

State that you will keep a record of assignments completed and not completed.

The policy should state that you will keep a daily record of all homework assignments completed and not completed. The fact that you will check all homework is enough to motivate many students to do their homework. Also, this type of record keeping says something to both students and parents about the value you place on each and every assignment.

Explain how homework will affect students' grades.

Students and parents need to know if homework will be graded separately or as a percentage of another grade. Some schools list homework as a separate item on report cards. Others consider homework as part of a citizenship grade or a subject grade. Whatever system you or your school uses should be stated in your homework policy.

For example:

- If a student has four or more "no credit" homework assignments in any one quarter, it will result in the final grade being dropped a full letter grade.
- Parents will be notified following the third "no credit" homework in any quarter.

Inform parents and students of test schedules.

It is important that parents and students know when tests will be scheduled and how they will be evaluated. The following is an example of a homework policy statement regarding tests for a math class:

"Tests will be given periodically, usually on a Wednesday or a Friday. Adequate notice will be given for all tests. To prepare for tests, go over notes and corrected homework assignments. Any test that receives a D or an F must be returned within two days signed by a parent. There will be no makeup of low quiz or test scores."

Note: Use the Test Update Slips (Appendix page 115) to inform parents and students of upcoming test dates.

Let parents know how you will positively reinforce students who complete homework.

Research has shown that positive reinforcement is useful in motivating students to do homework. Your homework policy, therefore, should include:

- Positive rewards for individual students: praise, awards, notes home to the parents.
- Positive rewards that can be earned by the entire class.

Chapter 7, "How to Motivate Students to Do Their Homework," will explain in detail how to use positive reinforcement to motivate students to do their homework.

Explain what will happen when students do not complete homework.

If students choose to do their homework, they will enjoy the rewards you have described to them. If they choose not to do their assignments, they choose to accept the consequences of that choice, such as the loss of certain privileges.

It is important to note here that in some instances students may be prevented from doing homework by circumstances outside of their control. You must be sensitive to your own students and their home situations. Students should not lose privileges for not completing homework when it is not their fault.

However, for most students it is not that they *can't* do their homework, it is that they *won't* do it. Simply saying that you expect homework to be completed every night is not enough. It is with these students who choose not to complete their assignments that you must back up your words with action. (See Chapter 8, "What to Do If Students Do Not Complete Homework.")

When students choose not to do their homework, you can take action such as:

- Have parents sign completed homework every night.
- Have parents sign an assignment sheet every night.
- Have students miss lunch break to complete homework.
- Have students complete homework in after-school detention.
- Lower students' grades.

Homework missed for legitimate reasons must be explained in a signed note from the parents.

Clarify what is expected of the parent.

Research consistently shows that parents are a key factor in students' achievement in school. It follows, therefore, that parents must play an important role in the homework process. Since you do not follow the homework and the students home, it is up to parents to provide the support students need to complete their homework appropriately. The homework policy needs to cover the specific type of support expected from parents.

You should expect parents to:

- Establish homework as a top priority for their children.
- Make sure that their children do homework in a quiet environment.
- Provide positive support when homework is completed.
- Not allow their children to get out of doing homework.
- Contact you if children have problems with homework.

While parents may agree in principal with all of these points, they may not know exactly how to go about providing the support you expect.

To help you gain the parental support you need, in Chapter 8 you will be given resource sheets to give to parents. These sheets give parents step-by-step instructions for what they must do to help solve the specific problem their child is having with homework.

Clarify what is expected of the student.

For students to meet expectations about completing homework, you must clearly define how you expect students to go about doing their assignments.
Typical expectations include:

- All assignments will be completed.
- Students will do homework on their own and to the best of their ability.
- Students will turn in work that is neatly done.
- Students will turn in homework on time.
- Students are responsible for making up homework assignments missed due to absence.

Clarify what is expected of the teacher.

It is important that students and parents understand your commitment to dealing with homework in the most effective manner possible. Your homework policy should let them know exactly what you will do to enhance that commitment.
For example:

- All homework will be collected and either graded or commented upon.
- Each homework assignment will have a specific learning objective in line with the goals of the course.
- Students will be told why they are doing specific assignments.
- Students will be informed of evaluation procedures and criteria.

How to Use the Homework Policy

If you have developed your own homework policy, give a copy to your administrator for approval. Some administrators may require that they have a copy on file. In any case, it's a good idea to share your plan with your administrator in case parents contact him or her with questions or problems. Your efforts cannot be supported unless your administrator knows what your plan is.

Discuss the homework policy with students.

At the beginning of the school year or whenever you begin the Homework Without Tears program, present your homework policy to your students and have a discussion regarding the guidelines. Make sure that students clearly understand what is expected of them in your class.

Send the homework policy home to parents.

Send a copy of the homework policy home to parents. It is important that all parents understand exactly what you expect of them and their children in the homework process. Send a letter home instructing the parents to discuss the information with their children. Provide a tear-off section on the accompanying letter for both parents and students to sign acknowledging that they have read and discussed the homework policy. Then have the students bring the signed portion of the letter back to you.

Sample Homework Policy

Dear Parent,

I believe homework is important because it is a valuable aid in helping students make the most of their experience in school. I give homework because it reinforces what has been taught in class, prepares students for upcoming lessons, and helps students develop self-discipline, responsibility and organizational skills.

Homework will be assigned Monday through Thursday nights, and should take students no more than one hour to complete (not including studying for tests and long-range projects.) Most homework assignments will involve reading chapters in the textbook, answering study questions and completing related worksheets.

Tests will be given periodically, usually on a Wednesday or a Friday. Adequate notice will be given for all tests. Any test that receives a D or an F must be returned within two days signed by a parent. There will be no makeup of low quiz or test scores. Students will have at least two week's notice to study for tests, and one written report will be assigned each grading period.

I expect students to follow these guidelines when completing homework assignments:
    All assignments will be completed.
    Students are responsible for making up homework missed due to absence.
    Homework will be turned in on time.
    Students will turn in work that is neatly done.

If students choose not do do their homework, the following consequences may occur:
    Parents will be asked to sign completed homework each night.
    Students will miss recess to complete homework.
    Students may be required to complete homework in after-school detention.

If a student has four or more "no credit" homework assignments in any one quarter, it will result in the final grade being dropped a full letter grade.

If there is a legitimate reason why a student is not able to finish homework, the parent must send a note on the day the homework is due stating the reason it was not completed. The note must be signed by the parent.

I feel that parents are the key to making homework a positive experience for their children. Therefore, I ask that they make homework a top priority, provide necessary supplies and a quiet homework environment, provide praise and support, and contact me if they notice a problem.

I am looking forward to enjoying an exciting, productive year at school. Please do not hesitate to call me if you have any questions regarding the homework policy or any other matter.

Sincerely,

Chapter 3
ESTABLISHING A SCHOOLWIDE HOMEWORK PLAN

Does this happen in your school?

- Teachers schedule tests without regard to anyone else's test schedule.
- Some students have very few homework assignments, while others have hours of work each evening.
- Students are overloaded with homework on some nights, and have none on other nights.
- Students—and parents—are not told when homework will be assigned.
- Students—and parents—are not aware of how work will be evaluated.
- Parents do not know how they can help their children with homework.

Schools that have an effective approach to homework start by developing a Schoolwide Homework Plan.

The purpose of a Schoolwide Homework Plan is the following:

To ensure that a written homework policy is sent home from each class.

To establish a schoolwide homework schedule designed to alleviate "homework overcrowding."

To establish a schoolwide testing schedule.

To assure that all students are taught the homework study skills necessary to do homework successfully.

To inform parents—through printed information, workshops, and regular communication from teachers—of their role in the homework process.

To provide for homework support systems such as Study Hall, Detention Room, Homework Hotline, Homework Helpline, etc.

Where to Start: Form a Homework Coordinating Committee.

A Homework Coordinating Committee should be composed of the principal, all department heads, the head of the counseling department, and vice principal. It will be the responsibility of the Homework Coordinating Committee to oversee the following:

1 Ensure that a written homework policy is sent home from each class.

2 Determine a schoolwide homework assignment and testing schedule.

3 Provide for the teaching of homework study skills to all students.

4 Establish regular lines of communication to parents about homework.

5 Organize and maintain homework support systems.

1 Ensure that a written homework policy is sent home from each class.

At the beginning of the school year, each student should receive a written homework policy for each class he or she attends. The policy should clearly state the rationale for assigning homework in the class. The policy should also let parents and students know when homework will be assigned, how often it will be assigned, how it will be evaluated and how it is to be completed. (See Chapter 2 for complete instructions on formulating a homework policy.)

Note: The Homework Coordinating Committee may determine some schoolwide standards regarding homework. These standards should be included in all teachers' homework policies.

2 Determine a schoolwide homework assignment and testing schedule.

To avoid the problem many students have of too much homework on certain nights, the Homework Coordinating Committee should formulate policy for specific nights on which different departments can assign "heavy" homework. Likewise, different departments can be assigned specific days of the week for scheduling major tests.

Note: Teachers should include these homework and test days in their homework policies.

3 Provide for the teaching of homework study skills to all students.

Making a commitment to excellence in your homework program means making a commitment to teach all students the skills they need to do homework successfully.

Chapter 5, "How to Teach Your Students to Do Homework Responsibly," provides a series of lessons that will teach students how to do homework in an organized, responsible, "take-charge" manner. These skills are crucial to students who will soon be taking on responsibilities both in higher education and in the job market.

For maximum effectiveness, the homework lessons should be taught at the beginning of the school year, prior to any homework being assigned. The Homework Coordinating Committee must be responsible for determining when and how the lessons will be taught. For example, the homework skills unit could be taught the first week of school by English teachers or by homeroom teachers.

4 Establish regular lines of communication to parents about homework.

Chapter 4, "The Home-School Connection," provides many suggestions for keeping the lines of communication open to parents. The Homework Coordinating Committee should take charge by:

- Requiring that a homework policy is sent home in each class at the beginning of the school year.

- Providing all parents with a copy of the reproducible Homework Handbook for Parents included in this book. (See Chapter 4.)

- Suggesting that teachers send home Monthly Assignment Calendars that list upcoming test dates, due dates and pertinent classroom information. (See page 113 of the Appendix.)

- Organizing, staffing and maintaining a variety of homework support systems (see below).

5 Organize and maintain homework support systems.

There are many ways that schools can help students and parents deal with the problems of homework. Here are a few suggestions:

Homework Hotline

Here's an innovative idea that's being used at Gunning Bedford Middle School in Delaware City, Delaware. Each day, teachers fill out a form that lists homework assignments for their classes. This information is then recorded on an answering machine. Students or parents can dial the "Homework" number and hear a playback of all homework assignments given that day. For students, it's an opportunity to get make-up assignments or to clarify assignments that were given. For parents, the hotline provides a means for checking to see if students have homework assignments. As a special bonus, the final portion of the tape is used to publicize current school activities. The Homework Hotline keeps everyone in touch.

Parent Workshops

Every parent gets frustrated by homework. It's probably been a battleground in most families for years. If you want parent support for the homework program, you must educate parents about why homework is important, and what they can do to help their children. Parent Workshops can bring parents and teachers together as partners in education.

Homework Helpline

A Homework Helpline, staffed by teachers or community volunteers, gives each student the opportunity of having a supportive, helpful hand when they need it. This is especially beneficial for students who are on their own after school and are having specific problems with a homework assignment.

Study Hall

Many schools set up homework study halls before or after school to address the needs of those students who do not have an appropriate place in which to do homework. These study halls are staffed on a rotating basis by teachers.

The guidelines for a study hall are:
- The room should be supervised by a teacher or other responsible adult.
- No talking; this is not a social hour.
- The students must work independently and only do homework.
- Use of the study hall is considered a privilege. If students disrupt, they will receive detention time or not be allowed the use of the study hall.

Note: We have included in this chapter only a sampling of the actions a Homework Coordinating Committee can take. A comprehensive Schoolwide Homework Plan might also include a system for schoolwide positive recognition for exemplary homework performance as well as a schoolwide plan for dealing with homework problems. Whatever actions the Homework Coordinating Committee takes, it should periodically review all components of the plan to assess effectiveness and pinpoint areas that can be improved.

Chapter 4
THE HOME-SCHOOL CONNECTION

Parent support is a key ingredient in the success of your homework program. It's up to you to let parents know that they are an important part of the homework process, and to give them the information they need to help their children succeed.

Follow these guidelines for increasing parent involvement:

Send home a homework policy at the beginning of the school year.

As discussed in Chapter 2, parents and students need to know exactly what is expected of them regarding homework responsibilities. A homework policy clearly defines the reponsibilities of everyone involved in the homework process—parents, teachers and students.

Provide parents with a copy of the Homework Without Tears Homework Handbook for Parents.

The Homework Handbook for Parents (pages 97-111 of the Appendix)) is a reproducible booklet that gives parents the information they need to help their children develop responsible homework habits.

The Homework Handbook includes:

Homework Tips:

        Set Up a Study Area
        Create a Homework Survival Kit
        Schedule Daily Homework Time
        Encourage Your Child to Work Independently
        Motivate with Praise

Study Skills Tips:

        How to Help with Long-Range Planning
        How to Help with Written Reports
        How to Help Your Child Study for Tests

Homework Management Forms:

Daily Schedule

Long-Range Planner

Written Report Checklist

Proofreading Checklist

Textbook Study Checklist

Parent-Teacher Communication Form

Student Schedule

How to use the Homework Handbook:

The reproducible pages of the Homework Handbook are located on pages 97-111of the Appendix. Run off a copy for each student to take home. (Ideally, the handbooks should be sent home at the beginning of the year, when the homework lessons are taught.) You may wish to add a cover letter explaining why you are sending the Homework Handbook (to provide parents with information that can help their children do homework more successfully). Include a tear-off signature portion to your letter. Ask parents to sign and return it upon receipt of the Homework Handbook.

Provide parents with communication opportunities.

Many parents are unsure about when or even *if* they should contact the teacher. Start the year off by letting parents know that you welcome their questions and concerns. Make sure that parents know where, when and how to reach you. Use the two-way Parent-Teacher Communication Form on page 114 of the Appendix when you wish to communicate in writing with a parent.

Parent-Teacher Communication Form

To: From:

Message:

Signature   Date

Reply:

Signature   Date

Send home monthly calendars that list upcoming projects, test dates, and special activities.

Parents can do a better job of helping their children organize their study time if they are aware of upcoming assignments. A Monthly Assignment Calendar is a good way to keep parents informed. Run off copies of the calendar on page 113 of the Appendix. Fill in the name of the month, corresponding dates, and add the following information:

- Test dates
- Project due dates
- Pertinent class information

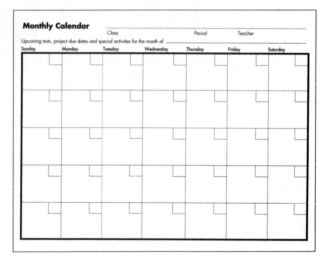

Monthly Calendar _____

Class _____   Period _____   Teacher _____

Upcoming tests, project due dates and special activities for the month of _____

Sunday	Monday	Tuesday	Wednesday	Thursday	Friday	Saturday

Send home Test Update Slips.

Parents need to know when tests are coming up. Students often need reminding, too. Use the Test Update Slips on page 115 of the Appendix to keep both groups informed. Send the slips home well in advance of important tests. (You will notice that some Test Update Slips have a space for both student and parent signatures. Use these slips when you want to make sure that parents have been informed of an upcoming test.) Have slips returned to class. This form of communication between home and school can be a very positive force in promoting good study habits.

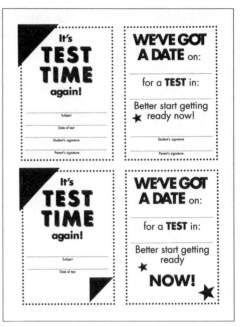

Send home Deadline Reminder Slips.

Tackling a big project successfully means breaking that project down into smaller steps, each with its own "mini-deadline." Help students hone their organizational and time-management skills by passing out these reminders (page 116 of the Appendix) when a deadline is coming up.

For example, Deadline Reminder Slips can be sent home as notification about these research report deadlines:

- preliminary outline due
- bibliography cards due
- note cards due
- final outline due
- rough draft due
- final draft due

Require students to use weekly assignment sheets.

A properly used assignment sheet is crucial to the development of a student's organizational skills. An assignment sheet also helps parents stay informed about what is going on in each class. Lesson 8 provides guidelines for using assignment sheets.

Send home study tips that parents can use with their children.

The Homework Handbook contains important study skills tips for parents to use with their children. As the year progresses, send home additional study skills information, particularly when it pertains to an upcoming assignment or project.

Chapter 5
HOW TO TEACH YOUR STUDENTS TO DO HOMEWORK RESPONSIBLY

Many students have difficulty with homework because they lack proper study habits and organizational skills. They don't do their work in an appropriate study area, they talk on the phone while doing homework, they forget to bring needed study materials home from school, and they don't understand what is expected of them on assignments.

This chapter gives you a series of lessons that will teach students how to do homework responsibly. The assignments contained in the lessons are designed to be the first homework assignments the students receive during the school year. If possible, the lessons should be presented in the first week or two of school. What the student learns from these lessons can then be applied to homework assignments the rest of the year.

Who should teach the homework lessons?

The goal of these lessons is to teach homework skills to each student within a grade level. To avoid repetition, not every teacher should teach these lessons. It should be the responsibility of the Homework Coordinating Committee (see Chapter 3) to determine who will teach the lessons contained in this book.

The Following Lessons Are Included in This Chapter:

Lesson 1: Accepting Responsibility: Putting Yourself in Charge of Your Homework
Lesson 2: Good Homework Habits Prepare Students
Lesson 3: Introducing the Homework Policy
Lesson 4: Setting Up a Study Area
Lesson 5: Scheduling Daily Homework Time
Lesson 6: Doing Homework on Your Own
Lesson 7: Rewarding Yourself for Homework Success
Lesson 8: Getting Organized with Assignment Sheets
Lesson 9: How to Schedule Long-Range Projects

Each lesson includes the following components:

A **Teacher's Lesson Plan** outlining the rationale, objective and procedure for the lesson. The lesson plans are contained within this chapter.

A **Student Worksheet** to reinforce and expand the lesson. Student Worksheet reproducible masters are in the Appendix section of this book.

To use the lessons in this chapter most effectively, first determine a time frame in which you will teach the lessons.

Note: All the lessons need to be taught together in the space of one or two weeks.

Follow this sequence when presenting each lesson:

- Read the lesson plan to familiarize yourself with the rationale, objectives and activities for the lesson.
- Make one copy for each student of the Student Worksheet(s).
- Teach the lesson to your students:
  - Introduce the concept.
  - Discuss the concept with your students.
  - Explain the homework assignment and distribute Student Worksheets.
  - Follow up as indicated on the lesson plan.

You are now ready to begin teaching your students to do their homework responsibly. Proceed to Lesson 1 on the next page.

Lesson 1
ACCEPTING RESPONSIBILITY: Putting Yourself in Charge of Your Homework

RATIONALE _____ To achieve success in school, students must understand that they are responsible for their own learning.

OBJECTIVE _____ After discussing the concept of assuming responsibility for learning, students will identify specific problems they have in getting homework done and come up with possible solutions to those problems.

MATERIALS _____ Student Worksheet 1 (Appendix pages 119-120)

Student Worksheet 2 (Appendix page 121)

PROCEDURE _____ **INTRODUCE THE CONCEPT OF ASSUMING RESPONSIBILITY FOR ONE'S BEHAVIOR**

1 Have individual students talk about where and how they assume responsibility in their own lives: Examples: jobs, schoolwork, chores at home.

2 Write some of the students' examples on the board. For each example, ask that student to explain the specific responsibilities involved.

Example:

- Responsibility: a weekly babysitting job.

- Responsibilities involved: being on time, feeding the children, cleaning up the house, keeping kids safe.

3 Tell students that as they grow older they can begin to understand that choices they make now can and do affect them in the future. This understanding can help them make more responsible choices in their actions. Returning to the examples listed on the board, ask the students what the future consequences might be for different ways of handling the responsibility.

Example:

Situation: Kara is due at her babysitting job in 5 minutes. Her boyfriend, Jeff, unexpectedly drops by. Kara knows she has to leave, but she'd really like to spend some more time with Jeff. It doesn't take Kara long to figure out the probable consequences for what she might decide to do.

- If I am on time to my babysitting job then:

    The parents (my employers) will be pleased; I'll feel good about myself; I'll probably be asked to work again. That means more money that I need. I'll be closer to getting the new dress I want.

- If I am not on time to my job then:

    The parents will be inconvenienced; They will probably be angry that I've let them down; I probably won't be asked to work again; I won't get the money that I need for my new dress. I'll feel bad about myself. I won't get referrals for more jobs.

By taking a moment to think about consequences, Kara can make a better, more responsible decision. Better for her in the long run, and better for the people who are relying on her.

Explain that making responsible decisions means looking ahead at the possible outcomes of your actions, and recognizing that your choices—your responses—will affect what happens to you! Assuming responsibility means being mature enough to understand that there are rewards to be earned--and consequences to be considered.

DISCUSS ASSUMING RESPONSIBILITY FOR LEARNING

1 Tell students that, just as they are assuming more responsibility for other things in life, they must also begin to accept more responsibility for learning. They need to recognize that they do have control over the choices they make about studying, homework, classwork. It's called "taking charge," and it can make a big difference. Accepting this responsibility means they can reap rewards or accept consequences. Taking charge means recognizing that it's up to the student. Tell students that one area they can take charge in is homework. From beginning to end, homework is up to them.

2 Brainstorm: In what ways can students take charge of their homework?

Examples:

- Get assignments done on time.
- Doing work on own.
- Planning time to get assignments done.
- Listening to directions in class.
- Take materials home.
- Do the best job I can.

3 Emphasize again that choices they make now affect them in the future. With this in mind, ask students to suggest some rewards that come from doing well with schoolwork.

Examples:

- Better grades
- Learning more
- Happier parents
- Happier self

4 What are some consequences for not doing well?

- Bad grades
- Can't be on sports team
- Feel bad about oneself
- Lose privileges at home

5 Tell students that taking charge of homework is not as tough as it might seem. It takes desire and planning. Students need to develop a plan of action. They need to recognize problems they have and take steps to solve them. Explain that in the upcoming homework lessons students will be looking at some of these problems and learning how to solve them.

EXPLAIN THE HOMEWORK ASSIGNMENT
(WORKSHEETS 1 and 2)

1 Tell students that you are giving them a homework assignment that will help them identify specific problems they have with homework. After identifying these problems they will choose some possible solutions.

2 Show Worksheet 1: Homework Headaches

Tell students that they are to write any problems they have with homework in the (squares) on the worksheet—one problem per square. After they write a problem, they are to brainstorm possible solutions to it. These solutions should be written in the surrounding ovals. Do a sample with the class. Ask students to name one homework problem. Write the problem on the board. Then brainstorm for solutions to the problem. Write these solutions on the board also.

Example:

Problem: Don't understand what I'm supposed to do.

Possible Solutions:

- Check over the assignment before leaving class.
- Ask the teacher for clarification if there's any problem.
- Call a friend.
- Ask parents if they can figure it out.

3 Show Worksheet 2: Homework Prescription: Take Charge!

Tell students that after they brainstorm and write solutions to their homework problems, they will select the solution(s) for each problem that they feel might really make a difference. They are to write this information down on Worksheet 2. Explain that this worksheet will be their own "plan of attack" for taking charge of their homework. Looking at the example on the board, choose the solution that seems to be most responsible, realistic, etc.

4 Tell students that they, and their parents, are to sign Worksheet 2 when it is completed. Explain that in a few weeks they will evaluate their plan to see how well it's working.

FOLLOW UP

1 **NEXT DAY** Collect the signed "Take-Charge Plans," check for completion and return to students. Tell them to keep the worksheet in their binders for future use. Explain that they will be adding new solutions to their sheets as they get new ideas from upcoming homework lessons.

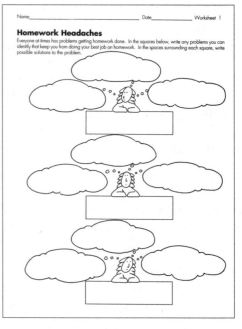

Lesson 2
GOOD HOMEWORK HABITS PREPARE STUDENTS

RATIONALE ⎯⎯⎯⎯⎯⎯⎯ Homework helps students develop skills they need to succeed both in higher education and in the job market. Homework encourages the development of self-discipline and independent work habits. It is important that students see the correlation between the responsible habits they develop now, and future job success.

OBJECTIVE ⎯⎯⎯⎯⎯⎯⎯ Students will take a "job skills" survey of two working people and correlate those skills to the skills they need to get homework done.

MATERIALS ⎯⎯⎯⎯⎯⎯⎯ Student Worksheet 3 (Appendix page 122)

Student Worksheet 4 (Appendix page 123)

PROCEDURE ⎯⎯⎯⎯⎯⎯⎯ **INTRODUCE THE CONCEPT OF RECOGNIZING THAT MANY IMPORTANT SKILLS ARE REQUIRED TO DO A BETTER JOB ON HOMEWORK**

1 Ask students to brainstorm all the different skills they use each time they complete and turn in a homework assignment. Start them off with one of the following examples. Write others on the board:

- Completing work on time.
- Planning time to do the work.
- Completing a job without being watched over.
- Having the supplies (resources) you need.
- Knowing where to get information you need.
- Can do work on own (accept responsibility).
- Doing your work correctly.
- Following directions accurately.
- Concentrate on a task.
- Work independently.

2 Now, referring to the list, ask students to give specific examples of how each of these skills helps homework get done.

Examples:

- Having supplies on hand means you don't get caught without lined paper the night before a written report is due.
- Working independently means that you don't need someone to always remind you that you have work to do.

DISCUSS THE RELATIONSHIP BETWEEN HOMEWORK SKILLS AND JOB SKILLS

1 Ask students why they think that these skills might also be called important life skills, skills that are important to develop for success in other areas of life.

2 Ask volunteers to tell about jobs they have been responsible for. (The jobs can range from babysitting to mowing lawns to regular employment at MacDonald's.) Which of the skills listed on the board were important in doing that job well?

3 Now ask students to give examples of different jobs they might want to do as adults. Again, correlate the job to the skills listed on the board.

EXPLAIN THE HOMEWORK ASSIGNMENT (WORKSHEETS 3 AND 4)

1 Tell students that you are giving them an assignment that will help them identify other the life skills.

2 Show Worksheet 3: Job Skills Survey

Tell students that they are to interview 2 working people. They are to write each person's job title and a description of the job and responsibilities. They are then to ask the person to check off all the skills listed on the worksheet that the person uses on the job.

3 Show Worksheet 4: Job Skills—Homework Skills

Tell students that, after completing the Job Skills Survey, they are to fill in the information on this worksheet.

Part 1:

Students are to choose a job they would like to have, now or in the future. They are to write a description of the job, then choose seven important job skills from the Job Skills Survey that would be important to doing this job well. Students are to list these seven skills and write why each is important to this job.

Part 2:

To complete this part of the worksheet, students are to check off all of the skills they used in order to do this homework assignment.

FOLLOW UP

1 **NEXT DAY** Discuss the results of the Job Skills Surveys. Have students read job descriptions and the skills that were checked off. What conclusions can be reached; what information learned? (For example: while there may be some differences in results, most jobs require that the worker be on time, be accurate, follows directions, has needed supplies, etc.

Name_____ Date_____ Worksheet 3

Job Skills Survey
Ask two working people to each complete the Job Skills Survey below.

Name of interview subject_____ Job title_____
Description of job duties_____
_____

Check off each statement below that applies to your job.

My job requires that I:
- [ ] show up on time.
- [ ] can complete a job without being watched over.
- [ ] can concentrate.
- [ ] do my work accurately, without many errors.
- [ ] know how to get information I need.
- [ ] plan my work so that it all gets done on time.
- [ ] know what supplies I need and have them on hand.
- [ ] know how to plan how long different tasks will take.
- [ ] accept responsibility for the work I do.
- [ ] follow directions accurately.
- [ ] complete work to the best of my ability.
- [ ] manage time.
- [ ] manage many projects at once.

Name of interview subject_____ Job title_____
Description of job duties_____

Check off each statement below that applies to your job.

My job requires that I:
- [ ] show up on time.
- [ ] can complete a job without being watched over.
- [ ] can concentrate.
- [ ] do my work accurately, without many errors.
- [ ] know how to get information I need.
- [ ] plan my work so that it all gets done on time.
- [ ] know what supplies I need and have them on hand.
- [ ] know how to plan how long different tasks will take.
- [ ] accept responsibility for the work I do.
- [ ] follow directions accurately.
- [ ] complete work to the best of my ability.
- [ ] manage time.
- [ ] manage many projects at once.

Name_____ Date_____ Worksheet 4

Job Skills—Homework Skills

Part 1: Choose a job that you would like to have, either now or in the future. Write a description of this job. Then, in the spaces below, list seven job skills that would be important to being successful at this job. Choose these seven skills from the list on the Job Skills Survey. Tell specifically why each would be important to the job.

Job Title: _____
Job Description: _____

Important job skills:	Why is this skill important to the job?
1 _____	_____
2 _____	_____
3 _____	_____
4 _____	_____
5 _____	_____
6 _____	_____
7 _____	_____

Part 2: What "job skills" did you use to complete this homework assignment. Check off each each box below that describes something you did to finish this assignment.

To complete this homework assignment, I:
- [ ] completed a job without being watched over.
- [ ] concentrated.
- [ ] worked accurately.
- [ ] got the information I needed.
- [ ] planned the work so it got done on time.
- [ ] had the supplies I needed to get the job done.
- [ ] scheduled enough time to finish the assignment.
- [ ] accept responsibility for my work.
- [ ] followed directions.
- [ ] did the work correctly to the best of my ability.

Lesson 3
INTRODUCING THE HOMEWORK POLICY

RATIONALE ——————— A homework policy establishes a firm foundation for homework by stating the expectations and responsibilities of everyone involved in the homework process—teacher, students, and parents. In Lesson 3, students will be introduced to your homework policy and learn exactly what is expected of them regarding homework.

OBJECTIVE ——————— After being introduced to the homework policy in class, the students will take home a copy of the policy, discuss it with their parents, obtain appropriate signatures, and return the signatures to school.

MATERIALS ——————— Homework Policy, Letter to parents

PROCEDURE ———————
INTRODUCE THE IMPORTANCE OF EVERYONE—TEACHER, PARENT, AND STUDENT—BEING INVOLVED IN HOMEWORK

1 Tell students that homework involves more than just the student. Explain that homework is a responsibility that involves the teacher, the students and their parents.

2 Ask students to tell what they think their own homework responsibilities might be. List their ideas on the board.

Examples:

- Bringing homework assignments home.
- Completing the assignments on time.
- Doing work neatly.
- Allow enough time to finish assignments each night.

3 Now ask students to talk about what their parents' homework responsibilities might be. List their ideas on the board.

Examples:

- Making sure that the student has a place to study at home.
- Helping the student get to the library when necessary.
- Reading and checking rough drafts.
- Helping the student study for tests.

4 Tell students that, as they get older, parents' responsibilities for their children's homework changes. Parents still need to be supportive. They still need to encourage their children, check on their work occasionally, and help when needed, but the student must really begin to assume the greater part of the responsibility. Explain that you will be sending home a Homework Handbook for Parents that will give parents information about when and how to help students.

> **Note:** This lesson has been designed to be used by the individual classroom teacher who is presenting his or her own homework policy. If you have a schoolwide homework policy, the homeroom teachers should be designated to teach this lesson.

DISCUSS HOW A HOMEWORK POLICY WILL HELP EVERYONE—TEACHER, STUDENT AND PARENTS—FULFILL THEIR RESPONSIBILITIES

1 Tell students that tonight you are going to give each of them a written homework policy to take home. Explain that a homework policy is a list of standards that will help students and parents understand their homework responsibilities. Read the policy to the class.

2 Explain why a homework policy is needed. (So that parents and students alike clearly understand your expectations about homework.)

3 Tell about the positives you will use when homework is done appropriately. Explain the consequences that will be imposed when homework is not done.

4 Check for student understanding by having them discuss the standards of the policy.

5 Give each student a signed (by you) copy of the homework policy and a cover letter to take home to parents.

EXPLAIN THE HOMEWORK ASSIGNMENT: TAKE THE HOMEWORK POLICY HOME, READ IT WITH PARENTS, AND RETURN THE SIGNATURE PORTION TO SCHOOL

1 Explain to students that they are to read the homework policy with their parents that night. Tell them that after reading the policy together, you want the students and their parents to sign the accompanying letter in the appropriate spaces. (Show the signature portion of the letter.) Explain that their signatures will let you know that parents and students understand what is expected of everyone regarding homework.

2 Tell students that you want them to return the signed tear-off portion of the letter to school the next day.

FOLLOW UP

1 **NEXT DAY** Collect signed papers. Review the homework policy once more to make certain that all students understand their responsibilities.

2 Put up a charted version of the homework policy in the classroom.

3 Do your part in enforcing the homework policy by always following through with your positives and consequences. Be consistent. Let your students know that in your classes homework is important.

Establishing a Homework Policy

Sample Homework Policy

Dear Parent,

I believe homework is important because it is a valuable aid in helping students make the most of their experience in school. I give homework because it reinforces what has been taught in class, prepares students for upcoming lessons, and helps students develop self-discipline, responsibility and organizational skills.

Homework will be assigned Monday through Thursday nights, and should take students no more than one hour to complete (not including studying for tests and long-range projects.) Most homework assignments will involve reading chapters in the textbook, answering study questions and completing related worksheets.

Tests will be given periodically, usually on a Wednesday or a Friday. Adequate notice will be given for all tests. Any test that receives a D or an F must be returned within two days signed by a parent. There will be no makeup of low quiz or test scores. Students will have at least two week's notice to study for tests, and one written report will be assigned each grading period.

I expect students to follow these guidelines when completing homework assignments:
    All assignments will be completed.
    Students are responsible for making up homework missed due to absence.
    Homework will be turned in on time.
    Students will turn in work that is neatly done.

If students choose not do do their homework, the following consequences may occur:
    Parents will be asked to sign completed homework each night.
    Students will miss recess to complete homework.
    Students may be required to complete homework in after-school detention.

If a student has four or more "no credit" homework assignments in any one quarter, it will result in the final grade being dropped a full letter grade.

If there is a legitimate reason why a student is not able to finish homework, the parent must send a note on the day the homework is due stating the reason it was not completed. The note must be signed by the parent.

I feel that parents are the key to making homework a positive experience for their children. Therefore, I ask that they make homework a top priority, provide necessary supplies and a quiet homework environment, provide praise and support, and contact me if they notice a problem.

I am looking forward to enjoying an exciting, productive year at school. Please do not hesitate to call me if you have any questions regarding the homework policy or any other matter.

Sincerely,

Lesson 4
SETTING UP A STUDY AREA

RATIONALE —————————— Students must understand that to do homework successfully, they must have a place in which to work. The study area must be well-lit, quiet, and have all necessary supplies at hand. Lesson 3 will give students the skills and motivation they need to set up a proper study area at home.

OBJECTIVE —————————— Students will complete a Study Area Survey and Homework Survival Kit Checklist . They will apply the information learned to choosing and setting up an appropriate study area at home.

MATERIALS —————————— Student Worksheet 5 (Appendix page 124)

Student Worksheet 6 (Appendix page 125)

PROCEDURE ——————————

INTRODUCE THE CONCEPT OF DOING HOMEWORK IN A STUDY AREA

1 Have individual students talk about where at home they usually do homework. Is this an effective place to work? What do they like about the location? What, if any, are some of the problems they have working in this location?

2 Share ideas about the following questions:

Should they do homework in a noisy room? Why or why not?

Should they do homework in front of a TV? Why or why not?

Should they do homework in the bus or car on the way home from school? Why or why not?

3 Ask students to brainstorm what a study area should be. Make sure that the following points are included: An appropriate study area is one that is well-lit, quiet, and has all necessary supplies at hand.

DISCUSS SETTING UP A PERSONAL STUDY AREA AT HOME

1 Encourage students to share ideas for study area locations in their homes. Ask these students to tell why the location would be a good place for doing homework.

2 Make it clear to students that even if they sometimes do most of their homework after school in another location (such as the library), they still need a place at home where they can study at other times.

3 Emphasize that the study area can be in any part of the home: kitchen, bedroom, living room, den, etc. It doesn't matter where it is as long as it's a place where the student can concentrate and get his or her work done.

4 Discuss the importance of making a personal study area FUN as well as FUNCTIONAL. Talk about setting up a study area in such a way that you want to use it—that it suits the way you study. Have students give examples of some "functional" things that might be in a study area.

Examples:

> desk or table, chair, lamp, wastebasket, supplies

Then ask students to give examples of "Study Area Additions" that can make doing homework a little more "comfortable."

Examples:

> a favorite poster, a doodle pad, photos of friends, a pillow
>
> **Note:** Recognize that some of your students may have real difficulty finding a quiet place to study at home. They may live in an overcrowded apartment, the environment may be unstable or chaotic, their parents may be unresponsive to their study needs, etc. Help these students explore study area alternatives. Talk about what they can do to help themselves by taking action on their own.

SOME SUGGESTIONS:

1 Find another place to do homework, such as the library or a friend's house.

2 Consistently ask their parents to support their study efforts by keeping sisters and brothers quiet during homework time.

3 Ask parents if one room can be off limits to others in the family during homework time.

4 Arrange with a brother or sister to do homework at the same time.

Be sure to ask students to give suggestions of their own to this problem.

DISCUSS THE CONCEPT OF CREATING A HOMEWORK SURVIVAL KIT

1 Tell students that an important part of getting homework assignments done each night is having all the supplies they need in their study area.

2 Ask students to talk about what happens at home when they can't find something they need in order to complete an assignment. (Example: A report is due the next day and they don't have a folder to put it in.) Share experiences of when not having the proper supplies really created a big problem for them.

3 Tell students that one way to solve this problem is by creating their own Homework Survival Kits. Explain that a Homework Survival Kit is a collection of all the materials they would need to do their homework.

4 Have the students list on the board some of the kinds of materials that should go in a Homework Survival Kit. Talk about whose responsibility it is to get these supplies. Have students suggest ways that the responsibility can be shared between parents and kids.

Example:

> The student can accept the responsibility for gathering those materials that are already available at home. He or she can also accept responsibility for making a list of items that should be purchased as soon as possible (pens, paper, pencils). The student could then approach parents with a proposal to purchase some items out of saved money; the parent could add to the money to purchase other items.

EXPLAIN THE HOMEWORK ASSIGNMENT (WORKSHEETS 5 AND 6)

1 Tell students that you are giving them an assignment that will help them set up a study area at home. Explain that their homework that night will be to complete a Study Area Survey.

2 Show Worksheet 5: Study Area Survey.

Tell students that they are to answer the survey information on the upper portion of the survey. Then, in the space below, they are to record information about the study area they are choosing at home. Remind students that they should talk to a parent about the study area choice, and to have a parent sign the completed worksheet.

3 Show Worksheet 6: Homework Survival Kit Checklist.

Tell students that you are giving them a list of the items that belong in a Homework Survival Kit. Emphasize to students that they—or their parents——are not expected to run out and buy everything on the list. Explain that a complete Homework Survival Kit is a goal, something to complete over time. Tell students that they are to have a parent sign the Homework Survival Kit Checklist and are to return it to school the next day. Tell students that their parent's signature on this worksheet means that the parent agrees to help the student put together a Homework Survival Kit.

Note: If some of your students do not have the means to obtain materials for a Homework Survival Kit, you can help by allowing them to take "portable" Survival Kits home from school. Let students take home specific materials they will need to complete a homework assignment (paper, markers, a pen, etc.). Have them carry these materials back and forth from home as needed. You might also check into the availability of supplies from school that could be given to students for the intent of helping with homework.

FOLLOW UP

1 NEXT DAY Collect the signed Study Area Surveys and Homework Survival Kit Checklists, check them off, and return them to the students. Tell students to use the Survival Kit Checklist to keep track of the items they already have at home, and those that they need to add as they begin to put together their own set of homework supplies.

2 TAKE-CHARGE PLAN UPDATE! Have students take out their Take-Charge Plan. Remind students that they have just completed a lesson on setting up a study area. They have learned what constitutes an appropriate study area, and what supplies should be available in the study area. Tell students to look over their Take-Charge Plan. Could working in a proper study area, or having needed homework supplies, be a solution to any of the problems listed on the page? If so, have students add this information to the "solutions" portion of the Plan.

Name_____ Date_____ Worksheet 5

Study Area Survey
Part 1
I usually do my homework in (name the location):_____

Briefly describe your study area. _____

These are the advantages of this study area: _____

These are the disadvantages of this study area: _____

Part 2
From now on I will do my homework in: _____

This location will be a good study area because: _____

I have agreed on this study area.

Parent signature

Student signature

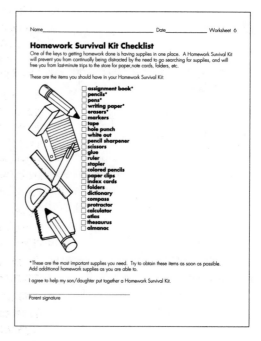

Name_____ Date_____ Worksheet 6

Homework Survival Kit Checklist
One of the keys to getting homework done is having supplies in one place. A Homework Survival Kit will prevent you from continually being distracted by the need to go searching for supplies, and will free you from last-minute trips to the store for paper, note cards, folders, etc.

These are the items you should have in your Homework Survival Kit:

- [ ] **assignment book***
- [ ] **pencils***
- [ ] **pens***
- [ ] **writing paper***
- [ ] **erasers***
- [ ] **markers**
- [ ] **tape**
- [ ] **hole punch**
- [ ] **white out**
- [ ] **pencil sharpener**
- [ ] **scissors**
- [ ] **glue**
- [ ] **ruler**
- [ ] **stapler**
- [ ] **colored pencils**
- [ ] **paper clips**
- [ ] **index cards**
- [ ] **folders**
- [ ] **dictionary**
- [ ] **compass**
- [ ] **protractor**
- [ ] **calculator**
- [ ] **atlas**
- [ ] **thesaurus**
- [ ] **almanac**

*These are the most important supplies you need. Try to obtain these items as soon as possible. Add additional homework supplies as you are able to.

I agree to help my son/daughter put together a Homework Survival Kit.

Parent signature

Lesson 5
SCHEDULING DAILY HOMEWORK TIME

RATIONALE _____ Homework—like other activities and responsibilities—must be scheduled into a student's life. Students must learn the time management skills that will enable them to do so. Lesson 5 will teach students how to schedule Daily Homework Time that is compatible with personal activities, and that also reflects their own best learning style.

OBJECTIVE _____ Students will record their daily after-school activities to determine a time each day for homework. They will apply the information learned in this activity to scheduling Daily Homework Time.

MATERIALS _____ Student Worksheet 7 (Appendix page 126)

PROCEDURE _____ **INTRODUCE THE CONCEPT OF SCHEDULING DAILY HOMEWORK TIME**

1 Ask students to talk about some of the problems they have had in getting homework done on time. Do they wait until late at night when they are too tired to do a good job? Do their parents "nag" them to get to work? Do other activities and responsibilities (sports, jobs, chores at home) ever interfere? Do social interests take precedence over homework?

2 Tell students that an important part of taking charge of homework is to schedule time for getting the homework done: a Daily Homework Time. Explain that Daily Homework Time is a pre-planned time set aside each day during which they will do their homework. Point out that the purpose of Daily Homework Time is to schedule homework into a student's life, just as other activities are scheduled. The goal of scheduling homework time is two-fold: to get homework done and leave time for pleasurable activities.

Note: Be aware of the particular needs of your students. Some students have no structure—or scheduled activities (other than school)—at all in their lives. Emphasize to these students that, just as knowing when school starts helps them get to class on time, Daily Homework Time will help them get homework done on time.

3 Tell students that there are two things to consider when setting up Daily Homework Time: (1) the external time patterns of already scheduled after-school activities and responsibilities and (2) their internal time patterns that help them know what time of day they function best for doing homework (e.g., right after school vs. after a social break).

4 Ask students to name some of the activities that are part of their external time schedules (sports practice, lessons, jobs). Do they usually get to these activities on time? Why do they think this is so? Reiterate that these activities are often taken care of on time because they are scheduled. Homework must also become a scheduled activity.

DISCUSS PERSONAL TIME PATTERNS

1 Ask student volunteers to tell what time of day they feel most mentally alert for homework. Right after school? After dinner? Later in the evening? Earlier in the evening?

2 Ask students why they think it's important to take into consideration their personal time patterns when deciding on the best time to do their homework.

3 Point out that if they are aware of their "peak hours" they can save that time for their most demanding homework tasks, and do easier work when they are not quite so energetic.

EXPLAIN THE HOMEWORK ASSIGNMENT (WORKSHEET 7)

1 Tell students that you are giving them an assignment that will help them schedule Daily Homework Time for one week.

2 Show Worksheet 7: Daily Schedule

Explain to students that they are to fill in all of their scheduled after-school activities and responsibilities in the spaces shown. Point out that by filling in all scheduled activities for a given week, they can clearly see what time is available for homework. Emphasize that students should also think about their personal time patterns. If, for example, Monday afternoon at 4 PM and Monday night at 7 PM are both available for Daily Homework Time, the students should carefully consider which time is best for him or her. Tell students to determine a Daily Homework Time for each day of the week and write it in the spaces shown.

Daily Schedule Write down all scheduled activities (music lessons, sports practices, etc.) and responsibilities (jobs, chores around the house, etc.) for each day of the week so you can clearly see what time is available for homework. Think about your personal time patterns and write in the best time for you to do homework each day. Mark your selected Daily Homework Time for each day in the spaces below.

Monday	Tuesday	Wednesday	Thursday	Friday
8:00	8:00	8:00	8:00	8:00
8:30	8:30	8:30	8:30	8:30
9:00	9:00	9:00	9:00	9:00
9:30	9:30	9:30	9:30	9:30
10:00	10:00	10:00	10:00	10:00
10:30	10:30	10:30	10:30	10:30
11:00	11:00	11:00	11:00	11:00
11:30	11:30	11:30	11:30	11:30
12:00	12:00	12:00	12:00	12:00
12:30	12:30	12:30	12:30	12:30
1:00	1:00	1:00	1:00	1:00
1:30	1:30	1:30	1:30	1:30
2:00	2:00	2:00	2:00	2:00
2:30	2:30	2:30	2:30	2:30
3:00	3:00	3:00	3:00	3:00
3:30	3:30	3:30	3:30	3:30
4:00	4:00	4:00	4:00	4:00
4:30	4:30	4:30	4:30	4:30
5:00	5:00	5:00	5:00	5:00
5:30	5:30	5:30	5:30	5:30
6:00	6:00	6:00	6:00	6:00
6:30	6:30	6:30	6:30	6:30
7:00	7:00	7:00	7:00	7:00
7:30	7:30	7:30	7:30	7:30
8:00	8:00	8:00	8:00	8:00
8:30	8:30	8:30	8:30	8:30
9:00	9:00	9:00	9:00	9:00
9:30	9:30	9:30	9:30	9:30
10:00	10:00	10:00	10:00	10:00

FOLLOW UP

1 NEXT DAY Check to see that students have completed their Daily Schedules. Tell them to keep these schedules close at hand. Encourage them to stick to these Daily Homework Times for one week.

2 TAKE-CHARGE PLAN UPDATE! Have students take out their Homework Take-Charge Plan. Remind students that they have just completed a lesson on scheduling Daily Homework Time. Tell students to look over their Take-Charge Plan. Could scheduling Daily Homework Time be a solution to any of the problems listed on the page? If so, have students add this information to the "solutions" portion of the Plan.

3 ONE WEEK LATER Ask students to complete the evaluation portion of the Daily Homework Time schedule. Briefly discuss the results in class. How many followed their schedules? Did it make a difference in getting homework done?

4 THROUGHOUT THE YEAR Make copies of the Daily Schedule available for student use.

Lesson 6
DOING HOMEWORK ON YOUR OWN

RATIONALE _____

Doing homework independently teaches a student responsibility and builds confidence and self-esteem. In Lesson 6 students will be encouraged to take pride in doing homework assignments on their own.

OBJECTIVE _____

Students will use "positive message" acronyms (e.g., A.C.E—Assignment Creatively Executed) to identify homework assignments that they are proud of having done—on their own and to the best of their ability.

MATERIALS _____

Student Worksheet 8 (Appendix page 127)

PROCEDURE _____

INTRODUCE THE CONCEPT OF DOING HOMEWORK ON YOUR OWN

1 Ask students to share ideas about why it's important to do homework assignments on their own, without a parent's or a friend's help. Stress the fact that although it may be easier to get work done if the student is always asking for—and getting—help, the student will not be learning. Point out that by doing homework on their own, and learning from the asignments, students will do better on classroom assignments, be able to contribute more to class discussions, and will be much more prepared for quizzes and tests. Also emphasize that by doing homework on their own they are learning to be responsible for themselves.

DISCUSS WITH STUDENTS DIFFERENT WAYS FOR THEM TO DO MORE OF THEIR HOMEWORK ON THEIR OWN

1 Brainstorm ways for students to do more of their homework assignments on their own.

Examples:

- Call a class "study buddy" if you need help in understanding or doing an assignment.

- Do the easiest parts of an assignment first so you feel successful. Tackle the hardest parts last.

- Ask for adult help only when you've tried it on your own and can't go any further.

- Make sure that all assignments are written down clearly on an assignment sheet. Before leaving class, ask questions if you're not sure what the assignment requires.

- Give yourself positive messages about how proud you'll be when you get the work done. (Example: "I really am a smart kid!")

EXPLAIN THE HOMEWORK ASSIGNMENT (WORKSHEET 8)

1 Tell students that you are giving them an assignment that will help them identify work they are proud of having done on their own.

2 Show Worksheet 8: A.C.E.

Tell students that each of the squares on this worksheet contains an acronym that is a positive message about a homework assignment. Tell students that they will use the squares to identify homework assignments that they are particularly proud of having done.

Be sure that students understand that an acronym is a word formed from the initial letters of other words. Here are some examples of well-known acronyms: MADD Mothers Against Drunk Driving; SADD Students Against Drunk Driving; N.O.W. National Organization for Women

3 Read the acronyms on the worksheet to the students:

A.C.E. Assignment Creatively Executed

W.O.W. Wonderfully Organized Work

E.S.P. Extraordinarily Superb Project

4 Point out that there are blank squares on the worksheet. Tell students that they are to invent a "positive message" acronym of their own for each of these spaces. Ask students to bring the completed worksheets back to school the next day.

5 Tell students that they are to cut out the acronym squares and keep them at home in their Homework Survival Kit. Tell students that you want them to use the acronym squares to identify future homework assignments that they are proud of having done independently. After all of the squares have been used up, students may simply write the acronyms on their homework papers.

FOLLOW UP

1 **NEXT DAY** Have students share the positive message acronyms they thought up. Keep a list of these acronyms and use them throughout the year to send positive messages back to students.

2 Make sure to give students feedback when they have used one of the acronym squares to identify a homework assignment. Make your comments relate to the acronym. (Examples: "You really ACED this project." "WOW! Great work!")

3 Use positive message acronyms as headliners for homework bulletin boards.

4 Encourage students to keep using this self-reinforcing system throughout the year.

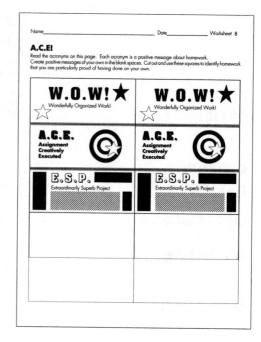

Lesson 7
REWARDING YOURSELF FOR HOMEWORK SUCCESS

RATIONALE

Praise received from others is a powerful motivator. But students must also learn to take pride in their own efforts and to give themselves a personal "pat on the back" when they are pleased with their accomplishments. Lesson 7 teaches students the importance of rewarding oneself for a job well done.

OBJECTIVE

Students will write a list of homework and study situations for which they might reward themselves. They will write suggestions of ways they can reward themselves and check them off whenever they do so.

MATERIALS

Student Worksheet 9 (Appendix page 128)

PROCEDURE

INTRODUCE THE CONCEPT OF REWARDING ONESELF FOR A JOB WELL DONE

1 Tell students that it's important to give yourself a pat on the back when you've done something you're particularly proud of. Talk about why it's important to recognize your own good efforts.

2 Ask students to tell of situations in which they've given themselves a reward for something they've done. Ask them how it felt.

3 Why is it a good idea to reward yourself?

DISCUSS WITH STUDENTS THE CONCEPT OF REWARDING THEMSELVES FOR DOING A GOOD JOB ON HOMEWORK AND STUDYING

1 Tell students that it's also a good idea to reward yourself for doing a good job with homework and studying. Explain that while it's true that working hard at school will bring rewards in the future (good grades, college, a better job, etc.) it is important to give oneself little "mini" rewards along the way. Those mini rewards can help get you through the most arduous study session!

2 Ask students to tell about different times that they might reward themselves. Examples:
- Each time I read (25) pages in my book report book.
- At the completion of each step in a long-range project.
- When I'm proud of the grade I got on a test.
- After each half hour of homework I complete.

3 Discuss each suggestion. Point out that it is particularly effective to give yourself a little reward during homework time each night. For example, after a half hour, or an hour, of homework is completed, a student might take 5 or 10 minutes out for a computer game, a brief chat on the phone, some stretching exercises or a snack. This reward time will serve two purposes: it's something to look forward to during study time, and it will clear your head and refresh you so you are better able to return to your work.

4 Now brainstorm ways students can reward themselves. Make sure that the students understand that these must be rewards they have the power to give themselves. Ask each student to suggest one reward that he or she would be able to give himself or herself.

Examples:

- Call a friend.
- Watch a television show when homework is completed.
- Fix a snack.
- Play a computer game.

EXPLAIN THE HOMEWORK ASSIGNMENT (WORKSHEET 9)

1 Tell students that you are giving them an assignment that will help them think about the different ways they can reward themselves for doing a good job on homework.

2 Show Worksheet 9: Reward Yourself! You Deserve It!

Point out that the worksheet contains a list of study situations for which students might want to give themselves a reward. Next to each situation, they are to list rewards that might be appropriate. (For example, a reward for completing a long-range project on time would probably be different than one given for doing a half hour of homework.) Emphasize once more that these rewards must be things that they really do have the power to give themselves. Tell students that after filling in their own mini-rewards, they are to track their use on the worksheet.

FOLLOW UP

1 NEXT DAY Collect and then return completed worksheets to students. Tell them to keep the sheet in their Homework Survival Kit as a reminder of ways to reward themselves.

2 TAKE-CHARGE PLAN UPDATE! Have students take out their Take-Charge Plan. Remind students that they have just completed a lesson on the importance of rewarding themselves for a job well done. Tell students to look over their Take-Charge Plan. Could a little "pat on the back" be a solution to any of the problems listed on the page? If so, have students add this information to the "solutions" portion of the Plan.

3 LATER Ask students to bring in their "Reward Checklist," Share different ways that students rewarded themselves. Ask students to evaluate the effectiveness of their "Study Reward System."

Name_____ Date_____ Worksheet 9

Reward Yourself! You Deserve It!

You don't have to wait for others to tell you you're doing a great job. You can do it yourself! In the spaces below, list study and homework situations for which you might want to give yourself a little reward. Next to each situation, write a reward that might be appropriate. Remember, these rewards must be things that you really can give yourself. Each time you give yourself the reward, check it off.

Study Situation	This is how I can reward myself.
Finished 10 math problems	
Read a chapter in social studies	
Wrote note cards on a chapter in science	
Finished a research paper!	

Lesson 8
GETTING ORGANIZED WITH ASSIGNMENT SHEETS

RATIONALE —————————— Often students' problems with homework can be traced to a lack of organizational skills. If students are to be more responsible for their own learning, they must be given the tools that will allow them to assume this responsibility. An assignment book (or assignment sheet) is a necessary organizational tool for students.

OBJECTIVE —————————— Students will complete a practice assignment sheet using abbreviations and speedwriting shortcuts.

MATERIALS —————————— Student Worksheet 10 (Appendix pages 129-130)

Student Worksheet 11 (Appendix page 131)

PROCEDURE —————————— ## INTRODUCE THE CONCEPT OF USING AN ASSIGNMENT SHEET

1 Ask students to talk about some of the problems that arise when homework assignments aren't written down properly. List their ideas on the board.

Examples:

- Students can't complete homework assignments because they don't remember what the assignment was.
- Students turn in homework assignments that are improperly done.
- Students do not plan ahead to allow for time to complete longer projects.
- Students forget about upcoming tests and quizzes.
- Students arrive home without the materials they need to complete homework assignments.

DISCUSS THE CONCEPT OF USING AN ASSIGNMENT SHEET TO WRITE DOWN ASSIGNMENTS

1 Tell students that they will be using (weekly or monthly) assignment sheets to record all homework assignments.

2 Ask students to discuss how using an assignment sheet might help them do a better job on homework. List their ideas on the board.

Examples:

- Provides one place where all homework assignments can be recorded.
- Provides a place to write down upcoming tests and project due dates.
- Students can look ahead to see upcoming due dates.
- Students can check the assignment sheet at the end of the school day to make sure they are bringing home all necessary materials.

3 Talk about some of the things students must keep in mind when writing down homework assignments. Share ideas.

Examples:

- Write complete information. (Writing "do problems 1-30 on page 68" isn't much help if the assignment really was to do only the even-numbered problems. Tell students that it's better to write down information rather than trust their memory.)

- Write down all materials needed to do the assignment.

- Write clearly and neatly.

- Use abbreviations and shortened forms of words whenever possible so that a lot of information can be recorded quickly in a small amount of space. (The homework assignment for this lesson deals with this concept.)

- Check assignments off as they are completed.

EXPLAIN THE HOMEWORK ASSIGNMENT (WORKSHEETS 10 AND 11)

1 Tell students that you are giving them an assignment that will help them learn how to fit a lot of information in a small space.

2 Show Worksheet 10: Speedwriting Shortcuts

Explain to students that one of the keys to writing complete information on an assignment sheet is to use abbreviations and other writing shortcuts. Point out that the worksheet contains a variety of "speedwriting shortcuts" that students can use when filling out assignment sheets. These shortcuts will save both time and space. Tell students that they are to complete the exercises on Worksheet 10.

3 Show Worksheet 11: Practice Assignment Sheet

Tell students that this part of the homework assignment will give them an opportunity to practice the speedwriting shortcuts they learned on Worksheet 10. Students are to read the assignments written at the top of the page, then rewrite them on the practice assignment sheet using abbreviations and other speedwriting shortcuts.

FOLLOW UP

1 NEXT DAY Go over the completed worksheets in class. Ask various students to write entries from the practice assignment sheet activity on the board. Compare methods used.

2 TAKE CHARGE PLAN UPDATE! Have students take out their Take-Charge Plan. Remind students that they have just completed a lesson on using assignment sheets. Tell students to look over their Take-Charge Plan. Could using an assignment sheet be a solution to any of the problems listed on the page? If so, have students add this information to the "solutions" portion of the Plan.

Name_____ Date_____ Worksheet 10

Speedwriting Shortcuts
When you write assignments on an assignment sheet, you have to get a lot of information into a small amount of space. You can make the job easier and faster by learning a few speedwriting shortcuts.

Speedwriting Shortcut #1
Use standard abbreviations when possible.

States, countries, directions, days of the week and months of the year all have familiar abbreviations. Here are examples of several standard abbreviations. Written next to each abbreviation is its definition.

ch.	chapter
e.g.	for example
etc.	and so forth
p.	page
pp.	pages

In the spaces below, write more standard abbreviations and their definitions. (You will find additional abbreviations listed at the back of a dictionary.)

_____
_____
_____

Speedwriting Shortcut #2
Use symbols when possible.

A symbol is a mark or sign that represents something. You can save a lot of space and time on your assignment sheet by using symbols instead of words.

Look at each symbol below. In the space given, write what the symbol represents.

$ _____		& _____	
+ _____		= _____	
? _____		< _____	
> _____		# _____	
@ _____		% _____	

Name_____ Date_____ Worksheet 11

Practice Assignment Sheet

Read the homework assignments written below. Then rewrite each one on the practice assignment sheet. Use speedwriting shortcuts to save time and space, but be sure to include all of the important information. Remember, there is not just one correct way to use abbreviations and shortcuts. Use what works best for you.

Math
Do problems 1-24 on page 68.
Show work on even-numbered problems only.
Review formulas in chapter 10.

English
Read chapter 4 in English book.
Do exercises 5 through 9.
Choose biography for book report by Friday.

Social Studies
Review chapter 10.
Answer questions 3, 6, 9, and 14 on page 124.
Watch "Crisis in Asia" on channel 4 tonight.
Final outline for research paper is due on Wednesday.

Spanish
Translate the paragraphs on page 46.
Oral presentation on holidays in Mexico due Monday, April 16.
Remember to bring Don Quixote to class tomorrow.

3 Pass out copies of the assignment sheets you want students to use. Tell students that they will be expected to record all assignments on this sheet. Clearly explain how you expect these assignment sheets to be filled in.

For example:

- Write all assignments in pencil (so they can be neatly erased and changed if necessary).
- Write test dates in red (so they'll stand out).
- Check assignments off as they are completed.

Give students a written list of assignment sheet guidelines listing your specific requirements.

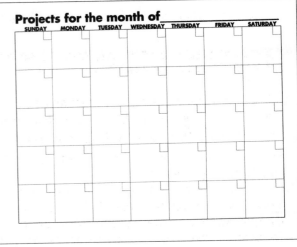

Note: In addition to weekly or monthly assignment sheets, students should also be provided long-range Project Planners. The Project Planner is used to write down upcoming project due dates and test dates. Give each student two copies of the Project Planner on page 132 of the Appendix. Have them fill in the appropriate names of the months and corresponding dates. Tell students to use these calendars to record important dates such as scheduled test dates, due dates for reports and anything else important that they'd like to remember.

4 Explain to students that their assignment sheets will be monitored. (To verify consistent, correct use of assignment sheets, it is important that they are checked on a regular basis.)

OTHER ASSIGNMENT BOOK OPTIONS

Include the assignment sheet as part of the student's grade. Grading the assignment sheet will encourage students to give it the proper attention. Make sure students understand your standards for grading the sheets, and what portion of the grade it will constitute.

Require parent signatures. Requiring parent signatures on assignment sheets is an excellent method of ensuring that parents know what homework is being assigned and when it is due. This is a particularly effective method to use with those students who exhibit an irresponsible attitude toward homework. Parent signatures can be required on a daily, weekly or monthly basis.

Lesson 9
HOW TO SCHEDULE LONG-RANGE PROJECTS

WHEN TO PRESENT THIS LESSON ——— Teach this lesson at the time you give students any long-range assignment such as a research paper, book report, or test study.

RATIONALE ——————— Long-range assignments are often the most difficult assignments students are asked to do. This is primarily because students lack the time-management and organizational skills vital to completing the work. Lesson 9 teaches students how to schedule all the steps of a long-range project so that the deadline can be met.

OBJECTIVE ——————— Whenever given a long-range assignment, the students will use the Long-Range Planner to break the assignment into a scheduled series of steps with a "mini-deadline" for each step.

Note: The process of learning to do a long-range project is as important to students as the final project itself. Keep in mind that your goal is for students to succeed. By assigning mini-deadlines for each step of the project, you can more effectively intervene and keep students on track, on time, organized and effectively learning the process of handing a long-range project, as well as producing a final product that meets the project goals.

MATERIALS ——————— Long-Range Planner (Appendix page 133)

PROCEDURE ———————

INTRODUCE THE CONCEPT OF BREAKING A BIG ASSIGNMENT DOWN INTO A SERIES OF LITTLE STEPS

1 Tell students that they are going to be working on a long-range project. (Describe the specific project: research report, book report, test study, etc.)

2 Ask students to recall the last assignment they had of this type. Ask how many students remember feeling overwhelmed by the project or felt a last-minute panic just before it was due.

3 Encourage students to talk about why they might have had these feelings. Examples:

- They didn't plan ahead.

- They waited until the last minute to begin work.

- All the research books were checked out of the library by the time they finally got started.

- There was so much to do they just didn't know where to begin.

4 Tell students that you are going to teach them to plan and organize their project so that they will learn to avoid these problems. Tell them that the key is to break the assignment down into a lot of little assignments, each with its own deadline.

DISCUSS THE LONG-RANGE ASSIGNMENT THAT YOUR STUDENTS WILL BE DOING

1 Describe the assignment in detail and give its due date.

2 Ask students to think about all the steps they have to do to get the assignment done. List ideas on the board. (Examples for a term paper: do research, check out books, write an outline, take notes)

3 Point out that, unless they organize all of these steps, it's very easy to get caught at the deadline without work being completed. For that reason, you and they are going to set up a series of mini-deadlines that will help them get the work done on time.

4 Write on the board (or show on an overhead projector) the steps you have determined are required to complete all parts of this assignment. (Your steps will most likely encompass all of the suggestions given by the students.) Do not write the steps in their proper sequence.

Note: The examples below show a hypothetical series of steps for three different long-range projects. These steps may or may not meet the particular requirements of your assignment, and are used only as an example. Determine the sequence of steps you want your students to follow for the long-range project before present this lesson.

Examples of Steps for a Written Report

Step 1: Pick out a topic for the report.

Step 2: Do research.

Step 3: Decide what questions you want to answer in the report.

Step 4: Take notes about the topic.

Step 5: Write the rough draft.

Step 6: Write the final draft.

Examples of Steps for a Book Report

Step 1: Choose a book.

Step 2: Read the book; Take notes as you read.

Step 3: Write a rough draft of the book report.

Step 4: Write a final draft of the report.

Examples of Steps for Studying for a Test

Step 1: Organize all test material.

Step 2: Make test study cards.

Step 3: Answer study questions at the end of the chapter.

Step 4: Review all material.

5 As a whole-class activity, have students sequence the steps of the assignment in their logical, proper order. Ask students to explain their reasons for the order. After the class is in agreement, have one student write the final sequenced list on the board for everyone to copy.

EXPLAIN HOW TO USE THE LONG-RANGE PLANNER

1 Hold up a copy of the Long-Range Planner. Tell students that using a Long-Range Planner before they do anything else on the assignment will help them schedule their project into smaller, more manageable steps. Explain that each of the steps listed on the board will have its own deadline. If they meet all these deadlines, then the final deadline should be no problem!

2 Distribute a copy of the Long-Range Planner to each student.

- Instruct the students to copy the steps for doing the long-range project from the board. Show them where to write the steps on the Long-Range Planner.

- Tell students to fill in the final due date on the last step they filled in.

3 Say to students, "Now let's come up with deadlines for each of the other steps. How long do you think it will take you to complete Step 1?" Share ideas and agree upon a deadline for the first step. Continue in this manner until deadlines have been set for each of the steps. Work back and readjust deadlines as needed, so that everything will be done by the final deadline.

4 Finish the lesson by emphasizing the importance of sticking to these mini-deadlines. Tell the students that you will be checking their progress at each deadline.

Note: See the "Deadline Reminder Slips" on page 116 of the Appendix. Pass these reproducible notes out to students to remind them of upcoming due dates.

5 Point out that below each "Due Date" space on the Planner there is a space for a parent's initials. Tell students that you will expect their parents to sign as each mini-deadline is met. The parent's initials will verify that the student has completed the step.

FOLLOW UP

1 Post a schedule of the mini-deadlines in the classroom. Tell students that on these dates you will be checking their work-in-progress. Explain that on these dates you will expect to see their Long-Range Planner signed by parents, and the current status of work done on the project.

2 Follow through by checking students' work at each mini-deadline. Provide plenty of praise and positive reinforcement as students meet these deadlines.

3 Give each student a supply of Long-Range Planners to keep in his or her study area. Encourage them to use the Long-Range Planner for any project that involves many steps and a lengthy period of time in which to complete it.

LONG-RANGE PLANNER

ASSIGNMENT _____

DUE DATE _____

1	_____ Due Date _____
	Parent's Initials _____
2	_____ Due Date _____
	Parent's Initials _____
3	_____ Due Date _____
	Parent's Initials _____
4	_____ Due Date _____
	Parent's Initials _____
5	_____ Due Date _____
	Parent's Initials _____
6	_____ Due Date _____
	Parent's Initials _____
7	_____ Due Date _____
	Parent's Initials _____

Chapter 6
5 STEPS TO GIVING EFFECTIVE HOMEWORK ASSIGNMENTS

Chapter 5 of this book provides lessons to teach your students how to do homework responsibly. But that's only part of the picture. The ultimate quality of your homework program—and its benefit to your students—depends upon the effectiveness of the homework assignments you give.

Homework is **not** effective when it is hastily assigned as students are walking out the door at the end of the day.

Homework is **not** effective when it has no learning objective.

Homework is **not** effective when it bears no connection to classroom lessons.

Homework is **not** effective when students do not have the necessary skills to complete it independently.

Keep in mind that each time you give a homework assignment you are asking you and your students to invest a great deal of time and energy. It is, therefore, extremely important that your homework assignments warrant this investment—and that time is being used to its maximum advantage.

What determines an effective homework assignment?

To be utilized as an effective educational tool, homework must be recognized as a *process*. The homework process begins when you first plan your classroom lesson. This is the time when you should focus on the objective of the homework assignment you intend to give. The process continues as you decide the *type* of assignment to give, as you create or choose that assignment, and as you introduce it to the class. The homework process doesn't end until the assignment has been collected, commented upon or graded and returned to the student.

Each step of this process is a vital component of an effective homework assignment.

To help guide you through the homework process, *Homework Without Tears for Teachers* provides these 5 Steps to Giving Effective Homework Assignments:

Step 1: Determine the learning objective of the homework assignment you are going to give.

Step 2: Make sure the homework assignment you choose fits the homework learning objective.

Step 3: Introduce the assignment to students clearly and effectively.

Step 4: Follow a pre-determined plan for collecting homework efficiently and in a time-saving manner.

Step 5: Utilize a variety of "Homework Correcting Shortcuts" for correcting homework.

STEP 1: Determine the learning objective of your homework assignment.

Before you give any homework assignment, you must first know exactly *why* you are giving it. To ensure that homework is more than busywork, you must clearly determine your learning objectives. You must ask yourself, "Why am I giving this assignment?"

Is your objective to have students **review and practice specific skills** or material learned in class?

Is your objective to **prepare** your students for an upcoming class topic?

Is your objective to have students **apply skills** or concepts learned in class to new situations?

Is your objective to have students **integrate a variety of skills** into a long-term assignment?

When you take time to determine the objective of your assignment, you help ensure the quality of that assignment by:

1 Giving yourself the opportunity to make sure that the learning objective is really worth pursuing. Are students going to learn from this task, or will they be filling their time and heads with unimportant facts or details?

2 Making sure that the learning objective is appropriate for all students.

3 Choosing or designing the type of assignment that would best fulfill the learning objective.

Note: Get into the habit of giving as much thought to your homework assignments as you do to your classroom lessons. The best time to plan your homework is when you are planning the lesson. Look at the homework assignment as an extension and enhancement of a specific lesson. Record your homework assignments in your planbook right alongside the day's lesson. Take time to evaluate the flow of homework. Is it leading somewhere, or is it simply a disorganized potpourri of tasks?

STEP 2: Make sure the homework assignment you choose fits the homework learning objective.

Your learning objective will determine the type of assignment you give. Homework assignments generally fall into four categories:

Practice Homework
Preparation Homework
Extension Homework
Long-term Homework

Practice Homework
Objective: To review and practice specific skills or materials covered in class.

Practice assignments are often the most commonly given homework. Because practice assignments can be readily given through supplemental materials as well as textbooks, they can also be the most easily misused and overused type of homework. Don't fall into the trap of handing out practice worksheets or drill work just to give out homework.

Keep in mind that your goal in giving a practice assignment must be to practice a particular skill that has been covered in class. Don't assign practice homework that is a conglomeration of lots of skills. For homework to be effective, the students must clearly see what skill they are practicing.

Examples of practice homework assignments:

"Write a synonym for each of the following words."
"Answer the review questions at the end of Chapter 6."
"Do the even-numbered problems on page 89."
"Conjugate the verbs *hablar*, *vivir*, and *tener* in the future tense."
"Circle the direct object in all of the sentences on page 49."

When should you assign practice homework?

Ask yourself: Is my learning objective to have students review and reinforce specific skills or material they have learned in class? Do the students *need* to practice this skill? Have they already mastered this skill?

Guidelines for Assigning More Effective Practice Homework Assignments

- Don't give practice assignments if students do not need to practice that skill.

- Make sure that the practice assignment covers material covered in class.

- Assign practice homework only after you have determined that students can do the work with reasonable success.

- Don't overdo drill assignments. Keep in mind that students who already grasp a concept don't need the practice, and would be better served and challenged by other types of homework. Likewise, students who don't understand a concept will just be reinforcing errors.

- Because it's sometimes difficult to be certain just who did a practice assignment (a friend, a brother or sister, or the student), it's a good idea to occasionally follow such assignments with a quiz to determine if learning is taking place.

- Avoid the temptation to hand out "last-minute" practice assignments just because you haven't planned anything else. Any homework is **not** better than no homework at all.

Additional Ideas for Improving the Effectiveness of Practice Homework

Assigning practice homework that matches your students' varied abilities and also raises their level of thinking need not require greater amounts of teacher preparation time. You can still give textbook assignments and utilize supplemental and workbook worksheets. However, *how* you use these materials is one of the keys to assigning more effective homework.

Here are some ways to use textbooks and workbooks creatively and at the appropriate level:

Math

- Instead of assigning all students the same 30-problem page, have each student select 5 or 10 problems on the page that show what they are able to do.

- Set a time limit that each student is expected to spend on a homework assignment and accept the number of problems the student does in that time. Have a parent signature verify the time.

- Have students complete a few math problems in their text and then write more of their own on the same concept.

- Ask students to do 1 or 2 math thought problems from the text, then make up 2 similar story problems based on situations from their own lives.

Language Arts

- Instead of defining spelling or vocabulary words, have students use the words in a poem or creative story.

- Have students select 12 words (for example) from a short story or novel they are reading. Give them specifics for choosing these words: words that describe how people feel, words that describe how things look, words that describe how things move, etc. Have students use these words creatively in their own writing.

Social Studies or Science

- Ask students to make up 5 questions about a chapter in a textbook that they think would tell whether someone really understood the chapter. Exchange questions with other students.

Preparation Homework

Objective: To prepare students for an upcoming topic.

Preparation homework is given when you want students to prepare on their own for an upcoming lesson. Properly assigned, preparation homework can serve to stimulate interest in the upcoming topic.

Examples of preparation homework assignments:

Language Arts

"Locate a book review in a magazine or newspaper. Cut out the review or make a copy of it. Read and evaluate the review and come to class prepared to discuss why the review would make you want to read or not read the book."

Social Studies

"Read about the upcoming election in today's newspaper. List three issues that the candidates are discussing. Be prepared to discuss these issues."

Health

"Watch the program *Earthquake* on channel 6 tonight. Be prepared tomorrow to talk about three different measures your family can take at home to prepare themselves for a large quake."

Science

"Read pages 189-204 in your science text. Be prepared to describe the function of the kidney."

When should you assign preparation homework?

Ask yourself: Is my goal to prepare students for an upcoming class topic? Will I follow up this assignment with related material in class?

Guidelines for Assigning More Effective Preparation Homework Assignments

- Make sure that your assignment is specific. Students must understand before they begin *why* they are doing this assignment.

- Always follow up a preparation homework asignment with a related lesson in class.

- Use a variety of materials for preparation homework assignments: newspaper, TV, magazines, interviews, etc.

Extension Homework

Objective: To apply concepts or skills learned in class to new situations.

The most meaningful and motivating learning occurs when students are asked to apply what they have learned in school to other situations. Homework, because it's done away from the classroom, provides the perfect opportunity for students to practice this transfer of learning. (A recognized goal of education is for students to be able to transfer learning from one context to another.) An extension homework assignment is one of the best uses you can make of homework. These assignments stimulate creative thinking and allow for individualized work at the proper learning level.

Examples of extension homework assignments:

Math

"Measure all the rooms of your home. Determine the square footage."

"Develop a food budget for a week for a family of four. Collect newspaper grocery ads to verify prices of what you will buy."

Language Arts

"Develop this scenario: The main character in (story currently being read) comes to school with you for a day. What would he or she think about the school? What would you talk about? What problems might arise? What would the visit be like?"

"Write a review of a book you have recently read. Then locate a review of the same book from another source. Compare opinions."

Social Studies

"Interview an adult who works for city or state government. Ask him or her to talk about . . . Prepare a list of questions prior to the interview."

"Interview a person newly arrived in the United States. Ask him or her to talk about . . ."

"Create a timeline of events concerning an ongoing current event (election, political issue, etc.)"

"Design a poster to interest tourists in visiting a specific country."

Health/Science

"Write down everything you eat for a week. Be sure to include all snacks, no matter how small. At the end of the week we will compare and evaluate eating habits."

"Interview your parent to find out what he or she typically ate each day as a child. Compare your parent's diet to yours."

"Develop a diet that would be suitable for people climbing Mt. Everest."

When should you assign extension homework?

Ask yourself: Is my goal to have students apply what they have learned in class to new situations?

Guidelines for Assigning More Effective Extension Homework Assignments

- Keep in mind that any subject matter is appropriate for extension homework.

- Brainstorm with students to come up with ways that they can apply what they've learned in school to other situations.

- Try to give extension homework as often as possible.

- See the Creative Homework Models (Chapter 9) for ideas for extension assignments. Start off with these lessons and you'll soon be coming up with lots more of your own.

Long-Range Homework
Objective: To integrate a variety of skills into a long-range project.

A long-range homework assignment requires the student to take many of the skills learned in class and build upon them to create something new. A long-range project requires the students to collect and organize information, turn that information into a different form, manage time, and enhance the project creatively. In short, a long-range assignment asks the student to "put it all together" to demonstrate a wide variety of skills.

Examples of long-range homework assignments:

- Book report
- Term paper
- Science project

When should you assign long-range homework?

Ask yourself: Is my goal to give students an assignment that requires them to utilize a variety of skills (including time management and creativity)?

Guidelines for Assigning More Effective Long-Range Homework Assignments

- Keep in mind that in a long-range project, the process is even more important than the final result. With assignments such as book reports, term papers, etc., your learning goals must also include time management and organizational skills.

- Long-range projects can easily overwhelm a student. Help your students break down a long-range project into a series of more manageable steps. (See Lesson 9: How to Schedule Long-Range Projects.)

- Set a series of interim deadlines to keep students on track.

- Be consistent in checking these deadlines.

- Teach students the skills they need to fulfill all requirements for the project: note taking, writing an outline, research skills, etc.

Additional points to keep in mind when designing and choosing homework assignments:

The homework assignment must not require the student to do something he or she does not know how to do.

Before a homework assignment is given, you must determine that each student has the skills (and, perhaps, resources) necessary to do the work. Keep in mind that most homework assignments are expected to be done independently. It makes no sense to give a student an independent assignment for which he or she lacks the skills to complete.

The assignment is not too much or too long.

Don't fall into the "more is better" trap. (This is particularly applicable to practice assignments.) Keep your objective for the assignment in mind. If, for example, 10 problems will let you know whether or not a student understands a specific math concept, why ask for 30? Remember, if a student grasps a concept, he or she doesn't need the practice. If the student does *not* understand the concept, he or she will just be reinforcing errors.

The written directions are clear and concise.

Few things are as frustrating to students as incomprehensible directions. Take time to re-read instructions. Make sure that expectations are clearly explained.

Homework time will be spent on *learning*.

Don't waste student time on non-learning tasks. For example, don't ask students to copy questions, *then* write the answers. They are not learning anything while copying. Instead, have them answer the questions in a complete sentence that explains what is being asked.

Homework should never be used as a disciplinary consequence.

Giving homework as a punishment is never appropriate. Remember that your homework goal is for learning to take place, and for the student to be a willing participant in that learning. When you assign homework as a disciplinary consequence, you identify this goal with a negative factor, and increase the likelihood that students will look upon homework with a less than enthusiastic response.

STEP 3: Introduce the homework assignment clearly.

How you present your homework assignments to your students can be as important to the effectiveness of the assignment as the type of homework you assign. Research has shown that the way homework is presented affects the frequency with which students complete the homework and the motivation of students to do a good job on their homework assignments.

You can improve the effectiveness of your homework assignments—and increase your students' homework achievement—by following the simple guidelines below:

Always discuss the purpose of each assignment by saying, "Doing this homework will help you to (for example) learn to use data from a table..." (Preparing for this step will also help *you* make certain there is a clear objective for the assignment.)

Give clear, concise directions both orally and in written form. Don't write the assignment on the board without discussion or explanation.

Write homework assignments in the same place each day. Designate a portion of the board as the "homework corner" and keep the assignment up all week so students who are absent can readily determine their make-up work.

Make sure you allow enough time for students to ask questions about the assignment. Don't wait until the last minute to give the homework assignment. Don't assume that students understand what is required of them just because they haven't asked many questions. To check on understanding, ask students to repeat the directions in their own words.

When appropriate, show samples of a successfully completed assignment to model what is expected or draw diagrams or pictures of what the final product should look like.

When appropriate, allow the students to start the homework assignment in class. If there is any confusion, the class can do a small part of the assignment together. You can help answer questions as they arise or ask students who understand the directions to model how they are doing the assignment.

When appropriate for the age and abilities of the students, give the class a list of homework assignments for the week. Let the students determine how to schedule their homework over the week. Or you can designate due dates for some of the priority assignments, allowing students to turn in the rest of the assignments at the end of the week. In this way, you'll encourage students to learn how to manage their own time and allow them flexibility in scheduling other activities.

Communicate your homework policy to the class on a frequent basis. Remind the students how the policy will be enforced when assignments are incomplete or late. Be consistent with consequences and make-up procedures, especially at the start of the school year when patterns are being set and with students who are testing the limits of your homework policy.

Continue to emphasize to students the importance of homework. Reinforce this importance by collecting and correcting all or most of the homework assignments.

> **Try other "homework helper" ideas to further ensure student success with homework.**

Institute a study hour after school.

Often students have trouble doing homework because they do not have an appropriate place in which to study. An after-school study hour can provide the quiet environment they need to complete assignments.

Assign a homework "study buddy" to each student.

Tell students to check with their study buddy when they are unsure of an assignment or need to work through a problem with someone else. A study buddy can also be a helpful aid in studying for tests.

Create a Homework Helpline for your class or school.

A Homework Helpline, staffed by teacher or community volunteers, gives each student the opportunity of having a supportive, helpful hand when they need it. This is especially beneficial for students who are on their own after school and are having specific problems with a homework assignment.

STEP 4: Use time-saving tips for collecting homework.

Finding efficient ways to collect students' homework assignments on a daily or weekly basis can save time and effort when it comes time to correct the homework. The suggestions that follow can be adapted to your own personal classroom style.

Have each student keep a homework file folder with his or her name on it. Each student should keep all completed homework in the folder at all times for daily, weekly or random checks.

Make a dated folder for each week's homework assignments. Staple a copy of each class list inside each folder so you—or the students—can quickly check off or initial who's completed the homework on time. In this way, you can immediately reinforce those students who have met homework deadlines while following through on consequences for those with late or missed assignments, per your homework policy.

Keep a "Homework Deposit Box" in class. Students put all completed assignments into the box before class begins, eliminating the need for using class time to collect work.

STEP 5: Use "Homework Survival Shortcuts" for correcting homework.

Research indicates that it is vitally important that you collect all homework and either grade it or comment on it. Not every assignment must be graded, but the students must know that homework will be checked and commented upon in some way. Finding efficient ways to correct students' homework assignments can help you give students needed feedback on a consistent basis and, at the same time, can give you relief from "homework burnout."

Keep in mind that you can always shorten your correction time by balancing the types of assignments you give:

- Easy-to-correct assignments vs. hard-to-correct assignments.

- Assignments that students correct vs. those that you correct.

- Assignments that require grades vs. those that need comments.

- Assignments with easy-to-check, definite answers vs. those that need comments.

- Assignments with easy-to-check, definite answers vs. assignments that are more open to your commentary or opinion.

In addition to balancing the types of assignments you give, you can also shorten your correction time by utilizing some or all of the "Homework Survival Shortcuts" listed in this section.

Note: Because these shortcuts involve techniques like random checks and correcting only one aspect of a paper, they should be explained in advance to students and parents so that there is no misunderstanding over what you are doing.

Explain to students and parents:

All homework assignments will be collected and either graded or commented upon. On occasion, the comments may center on only one aspect of an assignment. On occasion (especially with practice assignments) you may do a random check of the work. Reiterate to parents that the goal of homework is for learning to take place and that your job as a teacher is to determine if that is happening. As a professional, you have many techniques at your disposal, and the knowledge of when to use them appropriately.

> **Once explained, these time-saving techniques will help make homework a more positive experience for everyone involved.**

Caution: These Homework Survival Shortcuts should be used only after you have determined that appropriate homework habits have been developed (see Chapter 5, "Teaching Students to Do Homework Responsibly"). In addition, do not use these shortcuts when a brand new concept is being taught.

Choose problems or questions at random to correct and grade or comment upon. Check off the others to indicate how many items were completed.

Select key problems or questions and only grade or comment upon those. Check off the others to indicate how many items were completed.

Select only one or two criteria to grade or comment upon. For example, instead of always checking for the correct answers on math homework, quickly scan each student's paper to see if they showed their computations. Or, on written assignments, grade or comment on something new you taught the students about writing, such as using more active verbs or topic sentences with supporting details.

Give assignments that are appropriate for students to correct by themselves. Students may correct their own or another student's work. This technique saves you time and becomes a learning activity for the students.

The #1 Homework Correcting Rule

Whenever possible, comment in a positive way on how each student did on an assignment. Positive comments produce the best results! By commenting on the homework, you are letting students know that you place enough importance on their work to give it your time.

Summary

It is clear that the homework process requires a commitment from all involved. Assigning effective homework is your part of that commitment. When you take the time to ensure that the assignments you give are as effective as possible, you are ensuring in your classroom that homework means learning is taking place.

Chapter 7
HOW TO MOTIVATE STUDENTS TO DO THEIR HOMEWORK

Once you have taught students skills to help them take responsibility for their homework, you must provide motivation for students to complete homework on a regular basis.

For students who have had good school experiences and receive recognition at home, getting good grades may be motivation enough for them to do their homework. But the rest of your students may need something more to motivate them to complete homework. The most powerful motivational tool available to you is positive reinforcement.

Recognizing and rewarding appropriate behavior encourages students to continue that behavior. Students are more likely to continue to do homework when you give them praise for homework completed according to your expectations. A simple "Thank you for turning your homework in on time" can go a long way toward encouraging students to continue their good work.

Positive reinforcement can also change behavior. When you have students who occasionally do not do their homework, give them extra attention or special privileges on days when they do complete their assignments. With students who only now and then miss homework assignments, it is important to first concentrate on positives when they choose to do their work. Many times these students are just looking for attention. Therefore, make sure they receive more attention when they do their assignments than when they don't do them.

Also, by praising students for doing a good job on homework, you make them feel better about their own abilities. And as you increase students' confidence and raise their self-image, you encourage them to take responsibility for completing their work to the best of their ability.

Keep in mind the following guidelines:

Positive reinforcement must be:

- Something students like.
- Something you are comfortable using.
- Something used on a consistent basis.

Don't underestimate the power of positive reinforcement. Because of their home environment or previous experiences in school, many students lack and crave positive recognition. Your positive comments, notes and other incentives could be deciding factors in a student's self-confidence and success in school.

Positive Reinforcement You Can Give to Individual Students

Verbal praise

An effective form of reinforcement for doing homework is praise. Praise is appreciated by everyone. It is particularly important for those students who are hard to motivate. Many young people who do not do homework don't feel secure in their ability to succeed in anything relating to school. Keep in mind the enormous impact your praise can have on their self-esteem. With continual positive support, you can motivate students to develop a positive self-image and to approach homework with a confident, I-can-do-it attitude.

Use praise often, and remember:

- Praise should be specific. For example, "Chris, your use of descriptive words in your story was quite effective. I could almost feel myself in seventeenth-century France as I read it."

- To be most effective, praise must be used consistently.

- Give positive comments on the content of homework rather than just on the appearance.

- One-to-one praise is best so as not to embarrass the students in front of their peers.

Positive comments on completed homework

For many students, your consistent praise is enough to stimulate and sustain enthusiasm about homework. But others are more difficult to motivate with words alone. With these students, positive notes on their assignments can be very effective. When you check homework, add positive, specific comments not just at the top of the homework paper, but throughout the assignment.

Oftentimes, a note of praise from you is a much more powerful motivator than a good grade. Your notes can not only tell the students that you care about their work ("Sara, you put a lot of effort into this job. You really understood the assignment."), but can also let students know that you care about *them*. Remember, with hard-to-motivate students, building their self-esteem is key to helping them develop responsible habits.

Positive notes to parent

Students of all grade levels appreciate notes sent home to their parents recognizing that they have done a good job on homework. (See Appendix pages 134 and 135 for Positive Notes to Parents.) Also, if parents are fulfilling their role in supporting homework, they too will appreciate knowing that their efforts are paying off. It is important that you make contact with parents on a regular basis. When using positive notes to parents:

• Set a goal to send home a certain number of notes per week.

• Be specific with your praise. "Bob has been doing a terrific job turning all his homework assignments in on time. You should be very proud of his progress."

Have all students self-address special post cards that you plan to send to their parents.

Building a positive relationship with parents will also make it easier for you when you have to contact them about a problem. If you regularly send home positive notes, you communicate to the parents that you care about their children's success.

Second-Chance Bonus Paper

Students who have no late homework for a quarter earn the right to write another paper to replace one grade during that quarter. This second chance enables students to try to raise their grade, make up an assignment, or perhaps qualify for an athletic team or scholastic achievement.

The paper must be an improvement on the previous grade, clearly written and grammatically accurate to cancel the lower grade.

Homework Privilege Pass

Students who achieve homework goals established by their teachers and the school for a semester earn a Homework Privilege Pass (page 136 of the Appendix). The select group of students holding a Privilege Pass is permitted to move around the campus more freely.

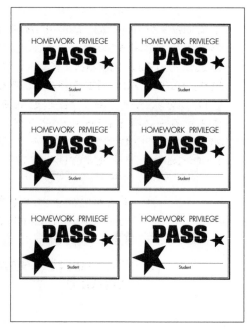

The pass, signed by the principal, allows them, for example, to enter the library at any time, gain extra computer time or additional athletic practice time, or be given a special parking place.

Homework Privilege Pass holders may also have their pictures posted so that all staff and students may know who they are.

Positive Reinforcement You Can Use for the Entire Class

Homework raffle

This reinforcement idea allows all students who complete their homework to have a chance at winning a raffle.

The students are told to put their names on both the left- and right-hand upper corners of their homework assignment papers.

When completed homework is turned in, tear off all of the right-hand corners and put them into a jar or box.

At the end of the week draw a name or two from the jar. The students whose names are drawn win a pass to miss a homework assignment or other special privilege.

Homework chart

You can set up a positive reinforcement system for the entire class by posting a homework chart on your bulletin board. The chart lists all of the students and provides a place to check every time a homework assignment is turned in on time. When the entire class (with the exception of those excused) turns in assignments on a given day, the class earns a point. When a certain number of points is earned, the entire class gets a night free of homework or another privilege. This system is also effective because of the peer pressure it creates for all students to turn in homework on time. The guidelines for using a homework chart are:

- Every time all students turn in a completed homework assignment, one point is earned by the class.

- When a predetermined number of points is reached, the class earns a reward.

Using a homework chart also gives you an excellent means of documentation of homework completed and not completed. Also, since the chart covers several weeks, it allows you to spot patterns where students continually have trouble completing homework on a certain day.

Bulletin boards to display student homework

Don't overlook bulletin boards as an effective motivator. By using a bulletin board featuring homework, you are giving the entire class a constant reminder of the importance you place on homework. Also, when you use the bulletin board to display homework that is done well, you are providing more positive reinforcement and a model of appropriate work. All students enjoy seeing their good work posted for everyone to see. When using a homework bulletin board:

- Introduce how you are going to use the bulletin board when you present your homework policy to your students. (To display the best papers in each class, etc.)

- Change the board weekly to allow as many students as possible to have their work displayed.

It doesn't have to take a lot of time to put together an eye-catching bulletin board. A large, clear headline backed by brightly colored construction paper will do just fine. Any "extras" you may want to add will enhance the overall effect.

Here are some sample bulletin board ideas to get you started:

Homework Hits!

Cut out "records" from black construction paper. Add colored "labels" and attach to the board as shown. Write the names of students who complete all homework for a week (or month) on records.

All-Star Homework

This sports-themed bulletin board can change throughout the year as the sports seasons change. Add photographs (from school sports events) or magazine and newspaper pictures to create interest. Attach blue ribbons to papers on display.

Homework Hall of Fame

For a "dignified" presentation, cut out columns from white construction paper, adding details with a black marker. Attach to the board, allowing for as much space as you wish. Attach gold seals to papers on display.

A.C.E. Homework!

(Assignments Creatively Executed)

This board is especially effective for displaying homework assignments that involve creativity.

Chapter 8
WHAT TO DO IF STUDENTS DO NOT COMPLETE HOMEWORK

If you consistently use the motivational ideas in the previous chapter and still have students not completing their homework, you must take further action.

However, before using any of the techniques described in this chapter, you must first determine if there are circumstances beyond a student's control that are preventing him or her from completing homework.

Your record keeping will help you identify sudden changes in homework that could indicate a problem at home. Of course, your first source of information is the student. When presenting your homework policy to the students, avoid a harsh "no excuses, no extensions" attitude and encourage your students to come to you if they have a problem getting assignments done.

Some students may be embarrassed to tell you that they couldn't do their homework because of chaotic conditions or other problems at home. If you suspect a problem, you may want to talk with the parents or other teachers to find out what the problem is.

The important thing to remember is not to arbitrarily take away privileges or lower grades when students do not complete their homework. Unfortunately, there are legitimate reasons why some students simply cannot complete their assignments at home. And if students feel they are being treated unjustly, they will soon begin to feel that nothing they do in school matters and resign themselves to failure. If you encounter students with problems such as this, listen to them and help them find solutions to the problem that is preventing them from doing homework.

If you determine it is the student who is at fault and is choosing not complete homework, then you should consider using the techniques presented in this chapter.

This chapter presents two approaches you can use to get all students to complete their homework.

- In Part One, you will be given techniques you can use at school with the students.

- In Part Two, you are provided resource sheets to give to parents to help them solve the most common homework problems.

Note: Any technique you plan to use with students who do not complete homework must be clearly explained in your homework practice statement.

Before using any disciplinary techniques for homework not completed, you need to ask yourself the following questions:

- Have you thoroughly explained homework assignments? Are the assignments appropriate to the student's grade level and have you determined that the student has the skills required to do the work successfully? (Review the guidelines in Chapter 6 on how to assign effective homework.)

- Has the student been taught the study and organizational skills required to do a successful job on homework?

- Are you sure that the student does not have a learning disability that is preventing him or her from completing homework?

- Are you sure that nothing has changed in the home environment to prevent the student from doing homework? (Has the student demonstrated ability in class to do a particular level of work but is unable to do it at home?)

- Do you collect and check all homework on a regular basis?

- Do you provide positive reinforcement on a regular basis?

If you have answered "yes" to all of these questions, and still have students who are not doing their homework, it is time for you to try the techniques suggested in this chapter.

PART ONE: WHAT YOU CAN DO AT SCHOOL WHEN STUDENTS DO NOT COMPLETE HOMEWORK

There are various techniques that are typically used by teachers with students who do not complete their homework assignments. We will give you examples of effective techniques, but you must choose those that you feel are appropriate for you and your students.

No matter what techniques you choose, you *must* have a means of keeping track of homework completed and not completed. Most teachers use their class record books to keep track of homework. It is important that you have these records available when contacting parents or enlisting the support of your administrator. You should also keep a record of notes sent home to parents and any disciplinary action (detention, etc.) taken with the student.

When determining the techniques you will use when students do not complete homework, keep in mind that the techniques must:

- Be described in your homework practice statement.
- Be something you are comfortable using.
- Be such that they apply equally to all students.

Homework assignment books

The most effective way to make sure all students do their homework is to have them write their assignments in a homework assignment book (such as Lee Canter's *Homework Organizer*). Students keep the assignment book in their notebook, take it home each day and bring it back the next day. If appropriate, you may ask parents to sign the assignment book each night, indicating that homework assignments have been completed.

Using an assignment book prevents students from saying that they don't know what their assignments are and ensures that the parents know exactly what is expected of their children each night. Simply involving parents with an assignment book will solve many problems because the students know that their parents know what each night's assignments are.

See Lesson 8 for guidelines on teaching students how to use an assignment book.

Lowering grades on assignment

Many teachers use lowering grades on assignments or overall subject grades to motivate students. If you use this policy, remember that the objective is not to fail students, but to see that the homework gets done. If the students feel that they are already failing, there is little incentive for them to mend their ways and choose to do their homework. If lowering grades is not effective in getting students to complete homework, contact the parents before giving students a failing grade.

The guidelines for using lower grades is as follows:

- The policy must be clearly explained to both students and parents before it is used.
- If students continue not to do homework, you must involve the parents.
- The policy must apply equally to all students.

Missed lunch

A common technique is to have students make up missed homework during lunch break.

If you use this technique, make sure that:

- Students finish their incomplete work by themselves.
- Talking is not allowed in the homework detention room.
- No assistance is given from a teacher or supervisor. This is not helping time.

Note: If a student is always spending lunch break doing homework, this may indicate a problem at home that is preventing him or her from working there. If you suspect this, it is time to involve the parents as suggested in the second part of this chapter.

Study hall or detention

Some schools set up homework study halls before school or after school that are manned on a rotating basis by teachers.

The guidelines for a study hall or detention room are:

- The room should be supervised by a teacher or other responsible adult.
- No talking; this is not a social hour.
- The students must work independently and only do homework.
- If students disrupt, they must receive additional detention time.

The most important point to remember is that no matter what techniques you use, you must use them consistently. You must use the techniques every single time a non-excused homework assignment is missed. Your students must realize that every time they choose not to complete homework, they are choosing to accept the consequences of that action. It is only if you take action every single time that your students will believe that you mean business.

PART TWO: WHAT PARENTS CAN DO AT HOME TO SOLVE HOMEWORK PROBLEMS

If problems with homework persist no matter what you do at school, you need more involvement on the part of the parents. And you must involve the parents in a way that will provide you with effective support at home. All too many parents are at a loss for what to do at home to ensure that their children complete their homework assignments. It is important, therefore, that you supply the parents with the knowledge and skills they need to deal with their children. Remember, all parents want their children to succeed. The more you help parents, the more they will be able to help you and their children.

Contact parents when you have a persistent problem with homework.

Probably the most common mistake in working with parents is that teachers do not contact them about a problem until the problem is out of hand. As soon as you realize a student is having problems with homework that necessitates involving the parents, *call them.*

Before contacting parents, plan what you will say.

Planning what you will say before contacting parents is essential to make sure that you are effectively communicating the situation. Make sure that parents understand that your number-one reason for calling is your concern for their child. When you show this concern, you maximize your opportunity to get parental support.

Follow these specific guidelines when contacting parents:

- **Describe the behavior that necessitated your call.**
  Describe in specific, observable terms what the student did or did not do. Phrases like "His homework is not acceptable" or "She is having a problem with homework" are not observable. Use comments like:

  "I am calling because I'm concerned about Angela's performance on homework assignments. She did not turn in three homework assignments this week, and missed two assignments last week."

  "I am calling because Brian consistently turns in homework assignments that are not complete."

- **Describe what you have done to help the student.**
  Clearly spell out that you have taken action on your own before contacting the parent.

  "*As stated in my homework policy*, I have praised your child when he does complete homework and had him come in at lunch time to complete unfinished work."

  "From your child's performance in class, I know she is capable of completing these assignments. I have discussed the problem with her and had her complete her assignments during lunch."

- **Describe what you want the parent to do.**
  Always preface what you want the parent to do with the statement, "It is in (name of student)'s best interest that we work together to help him (her). " For example:

  "It is in (name of student)'s best interest that she knows we are working together to help her complete all homework assignments. As she is having a recurring problem completing homework, I want you to support my efforts by taking away privileges like TV or talking on the telephone until her homework is done."

  Note: One option for parent action is to send home parent resource sheets that offer step-by-step solutions to some of the most common homework problems. (See page 74.)   If you choose to send a resource sheet home, make sure the parent understands how it is to be used.

- **Indicate your confidence in your ability to solve the problem if the parent works with you. Indicate that the parent's support is critical.**

  "I am sure that if we work together we will be able to motivate your son to get homework assignments done on time."

  "I am sure that if we work together we will most definitely help your daughter complete all of her homework assignments."

- **Indicate that there will be follow-up contact from you.**
  Let the parent know that you will not let the issue drop, and that you will be in touch within two weeks to inform the parent if the situation has or has not improved.

  "I'll be back in touch with you within two weeks, either by phone or with a note, to let you know how things are going."

If necessary, send home parent resource sheets.

To help parents deal with homework effectively, *Homework Without Tears for Teachers* provides you with resource sheets to give to parents to help them solve the most common homework problems. These sheets give parents step-by-step solutions to most of the homework problems they will face. These resource sheets can be found in the Appendix on the pages listed below and tell parents what to do if:

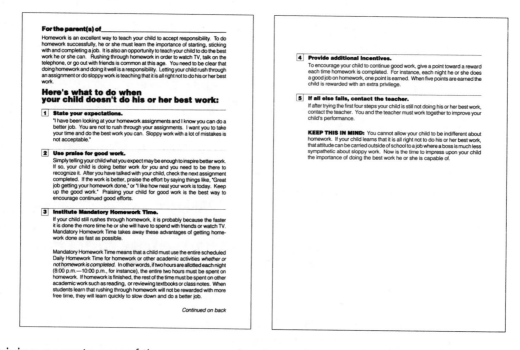

Before giving parents any of the resource sheets, make sure that you read them all thoroughly. While each sheet varies slightly, they all more or less give parents the following directions for solving their child's homework problem:

Parent resource sheets state that parents should:

1. Clearly and firmly state expectations to the child.
2. Institute Mandatory Homework Time (as explained on the resource sheets). Determine loss of privileges if child still chooses not to do homework.
3. Provide praise and support for continued good work.
4. Provide additional incentives for continued good work.
5. Back up their words with action.
6. Contact the teacher if all else fails.

How to Use Parent Resource Sheets

When there is a homework-related problem you need help with, contact the parents by phone or in a face-to-face meeting (see guidelines in this chapter for contacting parents by phone).

With the parents, discuss the problem the student is having with homework, (for example, takes all night to finish homework, forgets to bring assignments home, etc.).

Select the appropriate resource sheet and go over each of the steps to make sure the parents understand what is to be done. Then send the sheet home to the parents. Don't give the resource sheet to parents if you feel they will be intimidated by it. Just make sure they understand the steps they are to follow.

Set a time (in a week or two) to follow up with the parents to determine whether the strategy has been effective or if further action is necessary.

Summary

When dealing with students who are having problems getting homework done, remember that the most powerful technique you can use is positive reinforcement. Give them extra praise and recognition when they do complete homework responsibly.

If extra positives don't solve the problem, first make sure that there are not circumstances beyond the student's control that are preventing him or her from doing homework. If there are not, use techniques such as the ones suggested in this chapter to let students know that not doing homework is unacceptable. And whatever technique you choose to use, you must use it consistently every time a homework assignment is missed.

Chapter 9
CREATIVE HOMEWORK MODELS

The most meaningful and motivating learning occurs when students are asked to extend (apply) what they have learned in school to other situations in their lives. Homework, because it's done away from the classroom, provides the perfect opportunity for students to extend their learning.

The *Homework Without Tears for Teachers* Creative Homework Models supply a variety of formats for extension homework assignments in which *you* supply the content topic and the *students* apply what they have learned about that topic. The same Homework Model formats can be used over and over again in different subject areas with different content specifics.

See the examples below and on the next page:

Sample Language Arts Application

Sample Science Application

Sample Language Arts Application

Sample Social Studies Application

Each of the Creative Homework Models is designed at the extension (application) level to encourage students to really make learning relevant by seeing its application outside the classroom. As you examine the Homework Models, you will see that application of learning occurs when students role play, research, take a side on an issue, etc. The teacher's pages that follow describe each Homework Model format, show sample variations of use, and list many other suggestions for using the worksheets in different subject areas. The blackline reproducible pages are located in the Appendix, pages 147-153.

The Following Creative Homework Models Are Included in This Chapter:

Model 1: Role Play

Model 2: Pros and Cons

Model 3: Looking Into the Library

Model 4: Etcetera, Etcetera, Etcetera!

Model 5: Triple-Decker Homework

Creative Homework Model 1
ROLE PLAY

This homework sheet is designed to encourage students to put themselves in different roles—real and imaginary—based on characters from fiction and non-fiction stories and persons from their social studies, science and language readings.

BEFORE YOU BEGIN

Make a copy of the Creative Homework Model 1 worksheet (Appendix page 149) for each student in the class. Pass the worksheets out.

EXPLAIN THE ASSIGNMENT TO STUDENTS

Tell students that this assignment will give them the opportunity to role play or "put themselves in someone else's shoes." Share ideas about what that means. Tell students the assignment, write the assignment on the chalkboard, and have each student copy the assignment in the appropriate spaces on the worksheet. In order for students to "get into the role" ask them to close their eyes for a minute and imagine themselves "in that person's shoes" right now. Where are they? What does the world look like to them? How are they dressed? What emotions are they feeling? What are they thinking about? Suggest to students that they use this technique at home when working on this assignment.

APPLICATION

This activity can be effectively used in different subject areas. You can probably think of many ways to use this homework sheet that will fit your specific curriculum needs and homework learning objectives. Here are some examples:

Language Arts

Imagine that you:

- are best friends with the main character in a book you are reading. Write a journal page telling how the two of you one day changed the course of an important event in the story.

- are the author of the book you are reading. Write a journal page describing a typical day in your life.

- are the villain in a book you are reading. Write a journal page describing what events have caused you to be the way you are.

- are blind. Relying on your sense of hearing, smelling, feeling and tasting, write a journal page describing a day at the zoo (park, museum).

- are (name an author or poet you are studying). Write a journal page describing the events of the day that led you to write a specific work (story, book, or poem).

Creative Homework Model Worksheet 1

Name_____ Date_____

Role Play

Imagine that you *are the author of the book you are reading.*

Write a journal page *describing a typical day in your life.*

Science

Imagine that you:

- are (name a scientist you are studying). Write a journal page describing how you made one of your discoveries.

- are an astronaut on the first mission to Mars (or any other galactic destination). Write a journal page describing your first day on that planet.

- are a present-day scientist who has been transported back in time to the hospital where Florence Nightingale is nursing. Write a journal page describing one scientific discovery you would bring with you and tell how it might help or change things in the hospital.

- are a famous ecologist. Write a journal page describing how you helped save one endangered species from extinction.

Creative Homework Model Worksheet 1

Name_____ Date_____

Role Play

Imagine that you *are a famous ecologist*

Write a journal page *describing how you helped save an endangered species from extinction.*

Social Studies

Imagine that you:

- are the son or daughter of (name a famous world leader). Write a journal page describing your life. Tell about any responsibilities you have that are due to your parent's position.

- are a teenager living (name a country you are studying). Write a journal page describing a typical day in your country.

- are (name a president of the United States). Write a journal page describing the most important (eventful, terrible, infamous) day in your administration.

- are a teenager time-travelling to any other period of history. Write a journal page describing a famous person you would choose to bring back to your classroom.

- are a soldier in (name a particular war). Write a journal page describing a specific day during the war.

Creative Homework Model Worksheet 1

Name_____ Date_____

Role Play

Imagine that you *are a soldier in the Civil War.*

Write a journal page *describing a specific day in the war.*

Creative Homework Model 2
PROS AND CONS

This homework sheet is designed to help students think through the different sides of an issue or situation before forming their own opinion and stating their position.

BEFORE YOU BEGIN
Make a copy of the Creative Homework Model 2 worksheet (Appendix page 150) for each student in the class. Pass the worksheets out.

EXPLAIN THE ASSIGNMENT TO STUDENTS
Discuss the meaning of the word "opinion." Talk about the importance of recognizing that there is usually more than one side to any issue, and that these judgments are based on what a person believes to be true. Explain that before forming an opinion on *any* issue, it is best to first examine all sides of the issue. As an introduction to the homework assignment, briefly discuss a current issue in your school or community about which there is a difference of opinion. Have every student write down his or her own opinion, based upon previous exposure and personal beliefs. Then choose students to present all sides of the issue to the rest of the class. After all sides have been presented, discuss why final opinions may have been changed by examining everyone's input. Give students their assignment (see examples below). Write the assignment on the chalkboard and have students write it in the appropriate space on the worksheet.

APPLICATION
This activity can be effectively used in different subject areas. You can probably think of many ways to use this homework sheet that will fit your specific curriculum needs and homework learning objectives. Here are some examples:

Language Arts
List two reasons **for** and two reasons **against**:
- students addressing their teachers by their first names.
- teachers assigning homework on the weekends.
- young people having specific "chores" at home.
- students having weeknight or weekend jobs.
- students having to maintain a "B" average to participate in school sports.
- parents rewarding good grades with money.
- teaching students a second language, beginning in elementary school.
- dress codes in school.
- unannounced locker checks at school.

Creative Homework Model Worksheet 2

Name_____ Date_____

Pros and Cons

Inside the spaces below list two reasons **for** and two reasons **against** *parents rewarding good grades with money.*

Which argument do you favor? Explain your reasons.

Science/Health

List two reasons **for** and two reasons **against**:

- allowing motorcycle riders to drive between the lanes on freeways.
- requiring all students to eat a balanced lunch at school every day.
- showing beer and wine commercials on television.
- raising the driving age to 18.
- offshore oil drilling.
- a national health system.
- requiring the use of air bags in automobiles.
- legalizing certain drugs (marijuana, cocaine, heroin).
- a local environmental issue.
- selling "junk food" (candy, cookies, etc.) on campus.

Social Studies

List two reasons **for** and two reasons **against**:

- limiting couples to having only two children.
- a specific city, state, or national issue (such as legislators voting themselves pay raises).
- damming up rivers to make power plants.
- requiring all government workers to speak English.
- the Electoral College.
- providing election ballots in languages other than English.
- having a maximum age for the president of the United States.
- a specific historical issue (for example: the British tax on tea in 1773).

Creative Homework Model 3
LOOKING INTO THE LIBRARY

This homework sheet is designed to encourage students to use the library to find specific information on a wide variety of subjects.

BEFORE YOU BEGIN
Make one copy of the Creative Homework Model 3 worksheet (Appendix page 151) for each student in your class. Pass out the worksheet.

EXPLAIN THE ASSIGNMENT TO STUDENTS
Show students a variety of reference books that are available at the library—dictionaries, the encyclopedia, atlases, almanacs, the thesaurus, and the Guiness *Book of World Records*. Briefly explain the types of information that can be found in each book. Use this worksheet to expand upon textbook assignments or classroom discussions. Give students their assignment (see examples below). Write the assignment on the chalkboard and have each student write the assignment in the appropriate space on the worksheet.

APPLICATION
This activity can be effectively used in different subject areas. You can probably think of many ways to use this homework sheet that will fit your specific curriculum needs and homework learning objectives. Here are some examples:

Language Arts
Using the:

- thesaurus, rewrite a paragraph (from your reading book, textbook, etc.) using synonyms for 5 of the adjectives, nouns and verbs.

- thesaurus, rewrite the lyrics of a favorite song, using synonyms for as many of the words as you can.

- dictionary, define 5 words from your reading book (or an assigned poem or story) that you do not understand.

- Guiness *Book of World Records*, write down 5 interesting facts about (specify the subject).

- encyclopedia, write about the life and works of (name a specific author such as Shakespeare, Louisa May Alcott, Jane Austen, Edgar Allen Poe).

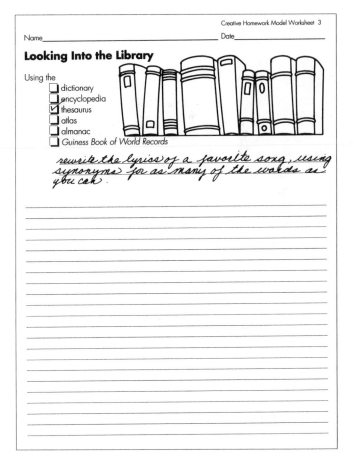

Creative Homework Model Worksheet 3

Name_____ Date_____

Looking Into the Library

Using the
- [ ] dictionary
- [ ] encyclopedia
- [x] thesaurus
- [ ] atlas
- [ ] almanac
- [ ] Guiness *Book of World Records*

rewrite the lyrics of a favorite song, using synonyms for as many of the words as you can.

Science/Health

Using the:

- encyclopedia, write three paragraphs about (name a specific scientist or field of science).

- almanac, list 8 scientific inventions, discoveries or theories that were developed in the 1700s (or any specific time).

- perpetual calendar in the almanac, list the day of the week on which Christmas occurred or will occur for the following years: 1860, 1900, 1919, 1950, 1975, 2000, 2010.

- *Guiness Book of World Records,* list the country with the oldest living trees, mountains, people.

- atlas, name the countries in Africa that have elephants, camels, gazelles, and gorillas.

Name_____ Creative Homework Model Worksheet 3

Date_____

Looking Into the Library

Using the
- [ ] dictionary
- [ ] encyclopedia
- [ ] thesaurus
- [ ] atlas
- [x] almanac
- [ ] *Guiness Book of World Records*

list 8 scientific discoveries or theories that were developed in the 1700s.

Social Studies

Using the:

- atlas, name 6 major cities on the Mississippi River.

- almanac, name the 10 largest islands in the world and the area of each in square miles.

- encyclopedia, write a few paragraphs on the development of the calendar.

- *Guiness Book of World Records,* name the country with the most Nobel Peace Prize winners.

- atlas, name the countries that border Peru, Nigeria, El Salvador, Israel and Switzerland.

Name_____ Creative Homework Model Worksheet 3

Date_____

Looking Into the Library

Using the
- [ ] dictionary
- [x] encyclopedia
- [ ] thesaurus
- [ ] atlas
- [ ] almanac
- [ ] *Guiness Book of World Records*

write a few paragraphs on the development of the calendar.

Creative Homework Model 4
ETCETERA, ETCETERA, ETCETERA!

This homework sheet is designed to help students form lists from specific subject area categories they are learning about in school.

BEFORE YOU BEGIN
Make a copy of the Creative Homework Model 4 worksheet (Appendix page 152) for each student in the class. Pass the worksheets out.

EXPLAIN THE ASSIGNMENT TO STUDENTS
Ask students to help you compile a list of the top music videos. Write each song on the board. Then ask each student to choose his or her favorite from the list. Explain to the students that they, too, will be compiling lists and choosing their preference from all the entries. Hand out the worksheet and explain that their homework assignment is to compile the most complete list they can on the specific topic. Suggest that they can use textbooks or other reference materials, but no "parental assistance" should be used. This is a purely "on your own" assignment. Explain that they may use the back of the sheet to complete the list, if necessary. Give students their assignment (see examples below). Write the assignment on the chalkboard and have students write it in the appropriate space on the worksheet.

APPLICATION
This activity can be effectively used in different subject areas. You can probably think of many ways to use this homework sheet that will fit your specific curriculum needs and homework learning objectives. Here are some examples:

Language Arts
List:
- words formed from the Latin roots -scrib- or -script- meaning "to write."
- compound words not in use before 1920.
- words which imitate the sound associated with them (onomatopoeia).
- similes (as stubborn as a mule).
- metaphors (He is a stick in the mud).
- acronyms (scuba—self contained underwater breathing apparatus).
- 5- (or more) syllable words.
- all the animals mentioned in the poem "The Unicorn."
- idioms (It's raining cats and dogs).
- all of the characters in a specific short story or poem.
- 20 adjectives that describe a specific character in a book.

Creative Homework Model Worksheet 4

Name_____ Date_____

Etcetera, Etcetera, Etcetera!

List _compound words not in use before 1920._

Circle your favorite. In the space below, explain why it is your favorite.

Math

List:

- prime numbers.
- things in a kitchen that could be measured using the formula $V = lwh$.
- things that number in the billions and above.
- things that are sold by the quart.

Social Studies

List:

- Vice presidents that have been elected to the presidency.
- present-day forms of transportation that could not have been used by Teddy Roosevelt (or name any other historical figure).
- the names of the men who signed the Declaration of Independence.
- countries with a population less than the city of Los Angeles.
- female heads of state (past and present).
- rivers that are tributaries of the Nile.
- states that are located completely above 40 degrees latitude.
- exports of (specify area).

Science/Health

List:

- animals that live only at the North Pole.
- rocks formed from volcanoes.
- meat-eating dinosaurs.
- items you should have in a first-aid kit.
- foods that are high in cholesterol.
- ways to recycle old clothes.
- animals that have become extinct in the last 20 years.

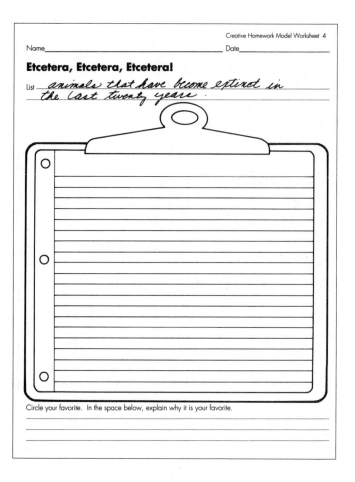

Creative Homework Model 5
TRIPLE-DECKER HOMEWORK

This homework sheet is designed to provide a creative way for students to do practice assignments. Each student selects specific problems on a given page that show what he or she is able to do.

BEFORE YOU BEGIN
Make a copy of the Creative Homework Model 5 worksheet (Appendix page 153) for each student in the class. Pass the worksheets out.

EXPLAIN THE ASSIGNMENT TO STUDENTS
With this worksheet, instead of doing all the problems on a given page, students choose those problems they feel most confident doing. This gives you an idea of what each student is and isn't capable of doing on his or her own. (Keep in mind that practice homework should only be assigned on material that has been previously covered in the classroom.) The worksheet specifies that problems must be chosen from the top third, middle third, and bottom third of the page. All you have to do is hand out the worksheet and assign the page number. Make sure that the students write this page number in the appropriate space on their worksheets.

APPLICATION
This worksheet is best suited for math practice homework. Here are some math skills that work well in this format:

- addition, subtraction, multiplication or division problems
- money problems
- word problems
- fractional number problems
- decimal fraction problems
- using the calculator to compute addition, subtraction, multiplication and division problems
- using the calculator to find square roots
- finding percents
- measurement problems
- using tools and devices (such as rulers and protractors) to answer questions
- algebra problems
- geometry problems

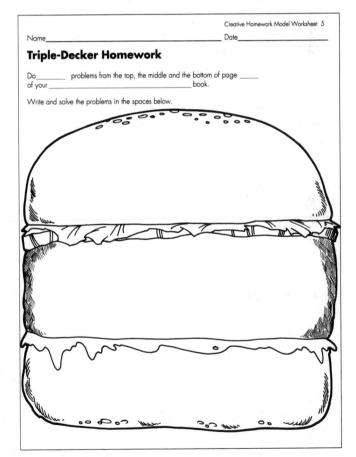

Creative Homework Model Worksheet 5

Name_____ Date_____

Triple-Decker Homework

Do_____ problems from the top, the middle and the bottom of page _____
of your _____ book.

Write and solve the problems in the spaces below.

CONCLUSION

There is no doubt that homework can be a valuable part of the education process for all involved. It can help students develop the study skills they need to achieve better in school and develop a sense of responsibility. Homework can provide a way for parents to be productively involved in their children's education. And for you, the teacher, homework can provide a valuable extension of the school day to reinforce your efforts in the classroom.

The key to making all of these benefits possible lies with you. All of the positive aspects of homework shrink to insignificance if the homework you assign is inappropriate for your students. The value of homework is relative. It is relative to the daily efforts you make to ensure that every homework assignment is meaningful and appropriate. But it is only with these efforts that you, your students and their parents can enjoy the rewards of homework completed responsibly, consistently . . . and without tears.

Homework Policy Planner

A **homework policy** establishes a firm foundation for homework by giving a rationale for homework and by stating the expectations for everyone involved in the homework process.

Answer the questions on this worksheet as they pertain to your homework objectives and practices. Use the information on this worksheet to help you write your own homework policy.

Why do you assign homework? In the spaces below, write your rationale for homework.
Example: Homework reinforces skills and material learned in class.

_____
_____
_____
_____
_____
_____

What types of assignments do you give in this class?

_____
_____
_____

How often is homework assigned?

_____
_____

What guidelines do you give students for when and how they are to complete homework?

_____
_____
_____
_____

How does homework affect a student's grade in this class?

_____
_____
_____

Do you positively reinforce students who complete homework assignments appropriately? If so, how?

_____
_____
_____
_____
_____

What steps do you take when students do not complete homework?

_____
_____
_____
_____
_____

What are the responsibilities of the student in the homework process? In the spaces below, list your expectations of students. Example: Students will turn in homework on time.

_____
_____
_____
_____
_____

What are the responsibilities of parents in the homework process? In the spaces below, list your expectations of parents. Example: Parents will provide students with a proper study environment.

_____
_____
_____
_____
_____

What are your responsibilities in the homework process? Example: All homework will be collected and either graded or commented upon.

_____
_____
_____
_____
_____

HOMEWORK HANDBOOK FOR PARENTS

Pages 97-111 of the Appendix contain the reproducible Homework Handbook for Parents. (Note: The pages of the Homework Handbook itself have been numbered from 1-15 to provide for easier use by parents.) The handbook is divided into two sections: Homework Tips, which gives parents guidelines for helping students make the most of their study time, and Study Skills Tips, which gives parents techniques for helping students write reports, study for tests, and plan long-range projects. The handbook also includes several Homework Management Forms that will help parents implement the tips.

Suggestions for Use

Run off copies of the Homework Handbook and send them home to parents at the beginning of the school year.

Attach a cover letter explaining that the Homework Handbook will provide parents with information that can help their children do homework more successfully. Include a tear-off signature portion of the letter. Ask parents to sign and return it upon receipt of the Homework Handbook.

Note: Depending on the age of your students and your particular homework needs, you may wish to send home sections of the Study Skills Tips portion of the handbook at a later date. For example, send home "How to Help with Written Reports" and the Long-Range Planner, Written Report Checklist and Proofreading Checklist when students are assigned a written report.

If your school has a schoolwide homework plan in place, it should be the responsibility of the Homework Coordinating Committee to oversee the distribution of the Homework Handbook to all students. Ideally, the handbooks should be sent home at the beginning of the year, when the homework lessons are taught.

HOMEWORK HANDBOOK FOR PARENTS

As a parent, it's important for you to know that homework really does make a difference in a student's performance at school. Research tells us that the time spent doing homework directly affects a student's achievement. This is important information. It tells us that by doing assigned homework, students will increase skills and do better in school. Here are some recent findings:

- Students who consistently do homework perform better academically than those who do not do homework.

- By doing homework, students can improve academic achievement in all subjects.

- Doing homework improves academic achievement of both high and low achievers.

When you help your child do homework appropriately, you are helping him or her improve academically *and* learn skills that will be beneficial throughout your child's life. Through homework, you have the daily opportunity to make your child more successful.

This Homework Handbook was designed to give you information that will help you guide your child toward responsible, independent study habits. Read the Homework Tips and Study Tips on the next pages. Each one can be incorporated into your child's study routine. The Homework Management Forms that are included at the back of the Handbook will help you implement these tips. This information, together with your interest and involvement, will provide the help and motivation your child needs to succeed.

HOMEWORK TIPS

Homework Tip #1
Set Up a Study Area

To do homework successfully, a student must have a place in which to work. The study area must be well-lit, quiet, and have all necessary supplies close at hand. A large space isn't necessary. The kitchen table or a corner of the living room is fine as long as it is quiet during homework time. Respect your child's study efforts by keeping brothers and sisters out of the way during homework time, and by keeping the TV and radio off.

Homework Tip #2
Create a Homework Survival Kit

One of the keys to getting homework done on time and without unnecessary hassle is having supplies all in one place. A Homework Survival Kit—containing supplies needed to do homework—will prevent your child from being continually distracted by the need to go searching for supplies, and will free everyone from last-minute trips to the store for folders, paper, tape, etc.

These are the supplies needed for a Homework Survival Kit:

pencils*	almanac
erasers*	markers
writing paper*	tape
pens*	rubber bands
assignment book*	hole punch
white out	scissors
glue	ruler
stapler	colored pencils
paper clips	index cards
dictionary	compass
atlas	protractor
calculator	thesaurus
pencil sharpener	

• Respect the Homework Survival Kit. Don't use these supplies for other family needs.

• Agree with your child that it is his or her responsibility to keep track of the Homework Survival Kit materials that are getting low and need replacing.

Remember, your child doesn't need to run out and get all of the supplies immediately. A completed Homework Survival Kit is a goal to work toward. Start by gathering the items marked by an asterisk (*). Get other supplies as you are able.

Homework Tip #3

Schedule Daily Homework Time

Homework, like other activities, must be scheduled into a student's life. Daily Homework Time is a pre-planned time set aside each day during which all homework must be done. During Daily Homework Time all other activities must stop; your child must go to his or her study area and get to work.

How to Choose a Daily Homework Time:

Have your child fill in all of his or her scheduled activities for the week on the Daily Schedule (page 9 of the Homework Handbook). Then, from the time available, have your child choose a Daily Homework Time for each day. Homework is to be done during Daily Homework Time.

Homework Tip #4

Encourage Your Child to Work Independently

Homework teaches students responsibility. Through homework, students learn skills they must develop if they are to grow to be independent, successful adults, capable of handling a job: how to follow directions, how to begin and complete a task, and how to manage time. By encouraging your child to work independently, you are helping develop these important life skills.

Homework Tip #5

Motivate With Praise

Everyone—no matter what age—responds to praise. Children need encouragement and support from the people whose opinions they really value the most--their parents.

Each night praise your child about some specific accomplishment. Say something positive about a specific goal your child has set and met. Example: "I really am proud of the way you have met your research paper deadlines. This rough draft is excellent!"

Use Super Praise to motivate your child

First, one parent praises the child: "I've noticed how hard you're working to do your homework each night. You're doing your work on your own and getting assignments done on time. I'll make sure Dad hears about this when he gets home."

Second, this parent praises the child in front of the other parent. "I thought you'd like to know Bob is doing a great job on homework. He's taking responsibility for his work, and completing it on time."

Finally, the other parent praises the child: "I'm really proud of you, getting such a good report from Mom. You're really doing great!"

If you're a single parent, you can use a grandparent, a neighbor, or a family friend as your partner in delivering Super Praise. Any adult whose approval your child will value can fill the role of the second person offering praise.

STUDY SKILLS TIPS

Getting homework done responsibly takes more than just wishing it to happen. Students need a quiet study area at home, a pre-planned homework time, consistent encouragement and motivation and, above all, a commitment on your part that homework is a priority in your home.

There's something else you can do to help your child. You can encourage him or her to develop study skills.

Study skills are techniques that enable students to learn more effectively. Knowing how to study is an important part of successful learning. But good study habits don't just happen naturally. They must be taught. Your child will be introduced to study skills in school. You can reinforce what is learned by encouraging the full use of these skills. The information presented in this part of the Homework Handbook can help.

The following study skills tips are included in this section:

- How to Help with Long-Range Planning
- How to Help with Written Reports
- How to Help Your Child Study for Tests

How to Help with Long-Range Planning

In addition to regularly assigned daily homework, students receive long-range assignments such as book reports, term papers, and studying for tests. These long-range assignments are often overwhelming because students do not know how to structure their time in order to get the work done. Too often, the bulk of the work is left to do at the last minute.

A Long-Range Planner can teach your child how to successfully complete longer projects. By using the the Long-Range Planner, your child will learn how to break down an overwhelming project into small, easily completed tasks. He or she will learn how to distribute the assignment over the period of time given for the project, and how to complete it on time. Make copies of the Long-Range Planner on page 10. Keep these copies handy for use whenever a long-range project is assigned.

Using the Long-Range Planner

When your child brings home a long-range project, take time to help him or her determine the steps that have to be followed to complete the project. Once the assignment has been broken down into more easily managed steps, work together to establish the time period in which each step will be completed. Write the steps and the dates of completion on the Long-Range Planner. See the example of a completed Long-Range Planner for a term report below. If each time goal is met, there will be no last-minute panic before the report is due.

Long-range projects are as easy as **1 2 3.**
1 Break down your BIG assignments into all of the smaller steps it takes to get the project done.
2 Write down "mini" due dates for each step.
3 Fill in the FINAL due date for the project on your last step.
Make copies of the blank Long-Range Planner to keep with your homework supplies.

LONG-RANGE PLANNER
ASSIGNMENT _Research Report_
DUE DATE _March 6_

1. Pick out topic. DUE DATE Feb. 2
2. Do research. DUE DATE Feb. 11
3. Decide what questions you want to answer in the report. DUE DATE Feb. 15
4. Take notes about the topic. DUE DATE Feb. 22
5. Write the rough draft. DUE DATE Feb. 29
6. Write the final draft. DUE DATE March 6
7. _____ DUE DATE

Make Copies

HOW TO HELP WITH WRITTEN REPORTS

Reports are often difficult for students to handle in an organized manner. Here are some tips that will help you encourage your child to perform at top capacity.

Tip #1 Use the Long-Range Planner

Planning is an important part of getting a written report done on time. If a term paper is left until the last minute, it is very unlikely that best-effort work will result. Using a Long-Range Planner will ensure that the project will be thought out and approached in an organized manner.

Tip #2 Use the Written Report Checklist

Before your child writes a report, encourage him or her to fill out a Written Report Checklist. (Make copies of the checklist on page 11 of this handbook.) By answering the questions on the checklist before starting to write, your child will prevent many unnecessary errors and rewrites.

Tip #3 Use a Proofreading Checklist

Proofreading is a critical step in completing any written assignment. You can help your child develop important proofreading skills by providing a Proofreading Checklist (see page 12 of this handbook). Make enough copies of the checklist so that there will always be plenty available at home. Make sure that your child understands that each draft of a written assignment should be proofread.

HOW TO HELP YOUR CHILD STUDY FOR TESTS

Step 1   **Determine what the test will cover and organize all study materials.**

Your child needs to know exactly what material a test will cover: chapters in the textbook, class notes, homework assignments, etc. Your child will study more successfully if he or she has organized all the materials that will be covered on the test and has them available for study.

Step 2   **Schedule time for studying.**

Your child needs to plan study time carefully to make sure enough time has been allowed to prepare for the test. Break down study tasks throughout week. It is better to study a little bit each day than to "cram" the night before a test.

Step 3   **Use effective study techniques.**

The following study techniques can help your child study more effectively:

Write important information on index cards.

A supply of 3" x 5" index cards should always be available at home. As your child studies, he or she should summarize important information and write it on index cards. Later, these index cards can be used to review for the test.

Review homework and class notes.

All homework and class notes should be reviewed before a test. It is helpful to underline or highlight important points.

Review study questions, past quizzes and tests.

It's always a good idea to look over past tests and quizzes. They might give clues about what to expect on future tests. Did the teacher ask multiple-choice questions? True/False questions? Essay questions? Was he or she interested in names and dates, or general trends? Make sure your child also spends time reviewing the study questions in the textbook. These questions provide an excellent review of the material covered.

Make a list of sample test questions.

Have your child make up a list of test questions that might show up on the test. Then have him or her prepare answers for these questions. Chances are, a lot of the questions *will* be given on the test.

HOW TO HELP YOUR CHILD STUDY FOR TESTS

PART TWO: HOW TO STUDY A TEXTBOOK

Often most of the material covered on a test will be from assigned reading in the class textbook. Here are some ideas that will enable your child to master the material in any textbook.

Step 1   Survey the chapter.

The first step in studying a textbook is to survey the chapter. Have your child follow these steps:

1   Make note of the headings of each main section.

2   Look over all pictures, maps, charts, tables and graphs.

3   Read the summary at the end of the chapter.

4   Read through the study questions listed at the end of the chapter.

5   Finally, go back and make up a question from each main heading. For example, if the heading is "The Magna Carta," you should ask, "What is the Magna Carta?" As you read the chapter (see Step 2) you will try to answer these questions.

Step 2   Read the chapter and take notes.

After your child has surveyed the chapter, he or she should go back and read it all the way through. Notes should be taken on a separate sheet of paper.

These notes should include:

• Answers to the questions formulated from the chapter headings.

• A chronological listing of events that occur in the chapter.

In addition, your child should take notes on index cards. Important facts (names of persons, terms to know, or significant concepts) are listed on the front of the card. The back should be used for listing important points that may be asked on the test.

Step 3   Review the chapter.

After your child finishes reading the chapter, he or she should look over the notes and make sure all the main points and how they interrelate are understood. Then your child should answer the study questions given at the end of the chapter, as well as the questions formulated from the main headings. He or she should review all the notes and all the key points of the chapter.

* Make copies of the Textbook Study Checklist on page 13 of this handbook. Give this checklist to your child for use when a test is assigned.

Daily Schedule

Write down all scheduled activities (music lessons, sports practices, etc.) and reponsibilities (jobs, chores around the house, etc.) for each day of the week so you can clearly see what time is available for homework. Think about your personal time patterns and write in the best time for you to do homework each day. Mark your selected Daily Homework Time for each day in the spaces below.

Monday	Tuesday	Wednesday	Thursday	Friday
8:00	8:00	8:00	8:00	8:00
8:30	8:30	8:30	8:30	8:30
9:00	9:00	9:00	9:00	9:00
9:30	9:30	9:30	9:30	9:30
10:00	10:00	10:00	10:00	10:00
10:30	10:30	10:30	10:30	10:30
11:00	11:00	11:00	11:00	11:00
11:30	11:30	11:30	11:30	11:30
12:00	12:00	12:00	12:00	12:00
12:30	12:30	12:30	12:30	12:30
1:00	1:00	1:00	1:00	1:00
1:30	1:30	1:30	1:30	1:30
2:00	2:00	2:00	2:00	2:00
2:30	2:30	2:30	2:30	2:30
3:00	3:00	3:00	3:00	3:00
3:30	3:30	3:30	3:30	3:30
4:00	4:00	4:00	4:00	4:00
4:30	4:30	4:30	4:30	4:30
5:00	5:00	5:00	5:00	5:00
5:30	5:30	5:30	5:30	5:30
6:00	6:00	6:00	6:00	6:00
6:30	6:30	6:30	6:30	6:30
7:00	7:00	7:00	7:00	7:00
7:30	7:30	7:30	7:30	7:30
8:00	8:00	8:00	8:00	8:00
8:30	8:30	8:30	8:30	8:30
9:00	9:00	9:00	9:00	9:00
9:30	9:30	9:30	9:30	9:30
10:00	10:00	10:00	10:00	10:00

Long-range projects are as easy as **1 2 3.**

1 Break down your BIG assignments into all of the smaller steps it takes to get the project done.
2 Write down "mini" due dates for each step.
3 Fill in the FINAL due date for the project on your last step.
Make copies of the blank Long-Range Planner to keep with your homework supplies.

LONG-RANGE PLANNER

ASSIGNMENT _____

DUE DATE _____

1 _____
_____DUE DATE_____

2 _____
_____DUE DATE_____

3 _____
_____DUE DATE_____

4 _____
_____DUE DATE_____

5 _____
_____DUE DATE_____

6 _____
_____DUE DATE_____

7 _____
_____DUE DATE_____

Make Copies

Whenever a report is assigned, take time to check off or write down the requirements. Don't forget to refer to this checklist when it's time to write the report. Be sure to **make copies** of the blank Written Report Checklist to keep with your homework supplies.

WRITTEN REPORT CHECKLIST

SUBJECT OF REPORT_____

DATE REPORT IS DUE_____

1 How long should the report be?
How many paragraphs____ or pages ____do I need to write?

2 Should the report be typewritten or handwritten?
Typewritten ☐   Pen ☐   Pencil ☐   Other ☐

3 Should I write or type on every line or every other line?
Every line ☐   Every other line ☐

4 Should I write or type on one side of the page or on both?
One side ☐   Both sides ☐

5 Where should I put the page numbers on each page?
Top ☐   Left ☐   Center ☐   Right ☐
Bottom ☐   Left ☐   Center ☐   Right ☐

6 Where should I put the heading on each page?
Top ☐   Bottom ☐

7 Should I put the report in a folder?
Yes ☐   No ☐

8 Should I add photos or illustrations?
Photos ☐   Illustrations ☐   Other_____

Use the Proofreading Checklist each time you complete a rough draft and again after your final draft. Be sure to **make copies** of the blank Proofreading Checklist to keep with your homework supplies.

PROOFREADING CHECKLIST

SUBJECT OF REPORT_____

DATE REPORT IS DUE_____

- [ ] The title of the paper is suited to the subject.

- [ ] The paper is well organized with a clear introduction.

- [ ] I have put in all capital letters, commas, periods and apostrophes where needed.

- [ ] Every sentence is a complete sentence.

- [ ] Each paragraph has a topic sentence that tells what the paragraph will be about.

- [ ] I have used descriptive words to make my paper more interesting.

- [ ] The paper contains specific facts and information about the subject.

- [ ] I have read my paper out loud, or reread it, and it says what I want it to say.

- [ ] The last sentence of the paper lets the reader know that the paper is finished.

- [ ] I have done at least one rough draft of the paper.

- [ ] I have checked the final paper for spelling errors.

- [ ] This is my best work.

Use this checklist to help you make sure you've covered all the important points of a chapter. Check off each item after you've completed it. First, be sure to **make copies** of the blank Textbook Study Checklist to keep with your homework supplies.

TEXTBOOK STUDY CHECKLIST

TEXTBOOK _____

CHAPTER _____

SURVEY THE CHAPTER

- [ ] Look over all major headings and subheadings.
- [ ] Note all pictures, maps, charts, tables, graphs, etc.
- [ ] Read the summary at the end of the chapter.
- [ ] Read the study questions listed at the end of the chapter.

MAKE QUESTIONS OF MAJOR HEADINGS

- [ ] Go through the chapter and reword all main headings into study questions to be answered.

READ THE CHAPTER AND TAKE NOTES

- [ ] Answer all the questions you made of the main headings.
- [ ] Take notes on a separate piece of paper.
- [ ] List important events, concepts or facts in order.
- [ ] Make 3"x5" index cards of important terms, people and events.

REVIEW THE CHAPTER

- [ ] Make sure you understand all the main points and how they relate to one another.
- [ ] Answer all the study questions at the end of the chapter.
- [ ] Review notes to make sure all key points have been covered.

Make Copies

Make copies of this communication form. If you have a question about homework, fill out the form, send it to school, and your child's teacher will get back to you with a reply.

Parent-Teacher Communication Form

To: _____   From: _____

Message:

_____

_____

_____

_____

_____

_____

_____

_____

_____

_____

_____

Signature _____   Date _____

- -

Reply:

_____

_____

_____

_____

_____

_____

_____

_____

_____

_____

_____

_____

_____

Signature _____   Date _____

Class Schedule

Have your child fill in the information on this sheet. Keep it available so you can contact any of your child's teachers as needed. Update the information as needed.

Period	Time	Class	Room	Teacher's Name
1				
2				
3				
4				
5				
6				
7				

Period	Time	Class	Room	Teacher's Name
1				
2				
3				
4				
5				
6				
7				

Period	Time	Class	Room	Teacher's Name
1				
2				
3				
4				
5				
6				
7				

Monthly Calendar

Class _____ Period _____ Teacher _____

Upcoming tests, project due dates and special activities for the month of _____

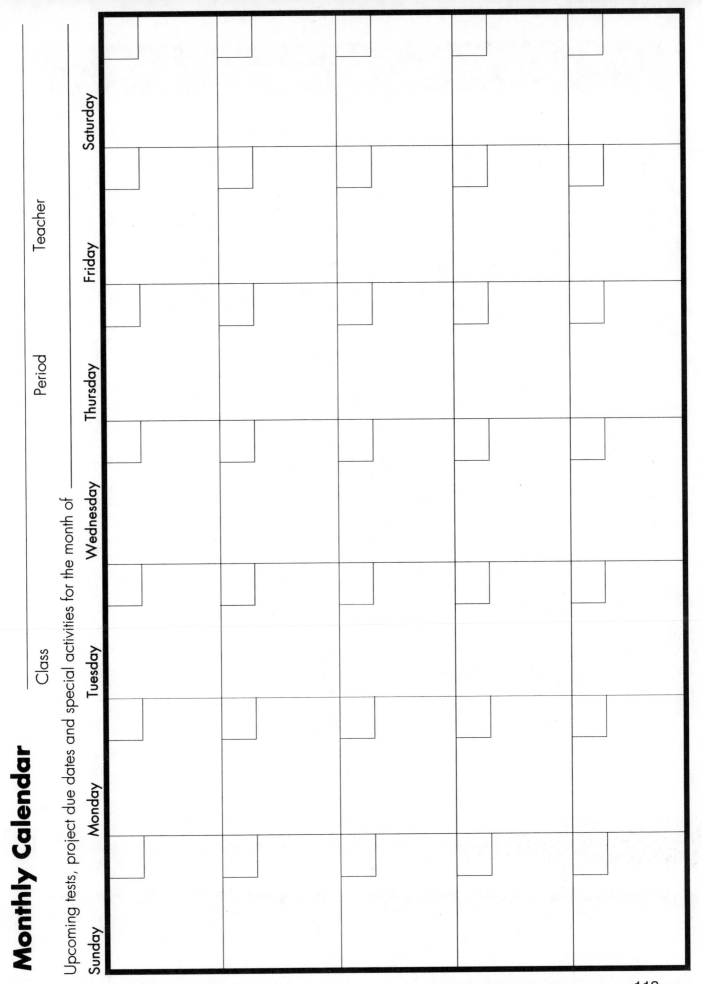

Sunday	Monday	Tuesday	Wednesday	Thursday	Friday	Saturday

Parent-Teacher Communication Form

To: From:

Message:

Signature   Date

- -

Reply:

Signature   Date

It's
TEST
TIME
again!

_____
Subject

_____
Date of test

_____
Student's signature

_____
Parent's signature

WE'VE GOT
A DATE on:

_____

for a **TEST** in:

_____

Better start getting
★ ready now!

_____
Student's signature

_____
Parent's signature

It's
TEST
TIME
again!

_____
Subject

_____
Date of test

WE'VE GOT
A DATE on:

_____

for a **TEST** in:

_____

Better start getting
ready
★
NOW!

Don't forget!

_____

is due

_____

Just a little reminder.
Your
resource list
is due

_____

P.S.
Your first outline
is due

_____

Thank You!

Upcoming Event!
Note cards are due

_____

Please have them
completed!

First Draft
is due

_____

Then it's all
downhill!

Outline Update!
Your final outline
is due

_____

Don't be late!

News Flash!
**Bibliography
due on**

_____

Wow!

Countdown to Completion!
Your revised, rewritten
final copy is due on

_____

STUDENT WORKSHEETS FOR HOMEWORK LESSONS

Pages 119-133 of the Appendix contain the reproducible Student Worksheets that correspond to the homework lessons provided in Chapter 5, "How to Teach Your Students to Do Homework Responsibly." Each of these worksheets has been designed to both reinforce the learning objective of the lesson, and to extend that learning into real application. Keep in mind that all of these homework lessons should be presented within a two-week time period. Therefore, it would be helpful to run off copies of all worksheets (one per student of each worksheet) before you begin teaching the homework unit.

Student Worksheets:

Homework Headaches

Everyone at times has problems getting homework done. In the squares below, write any problems you can identify that keep you from doing your best job on homework. In the spaces surrounding each square, write possible solutions to the problem.

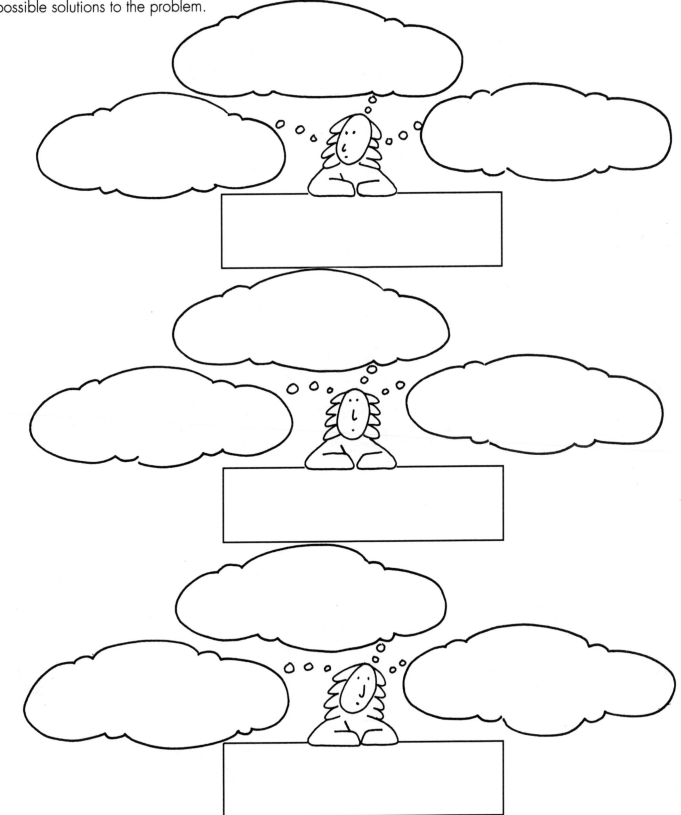

Homework Headaches continued

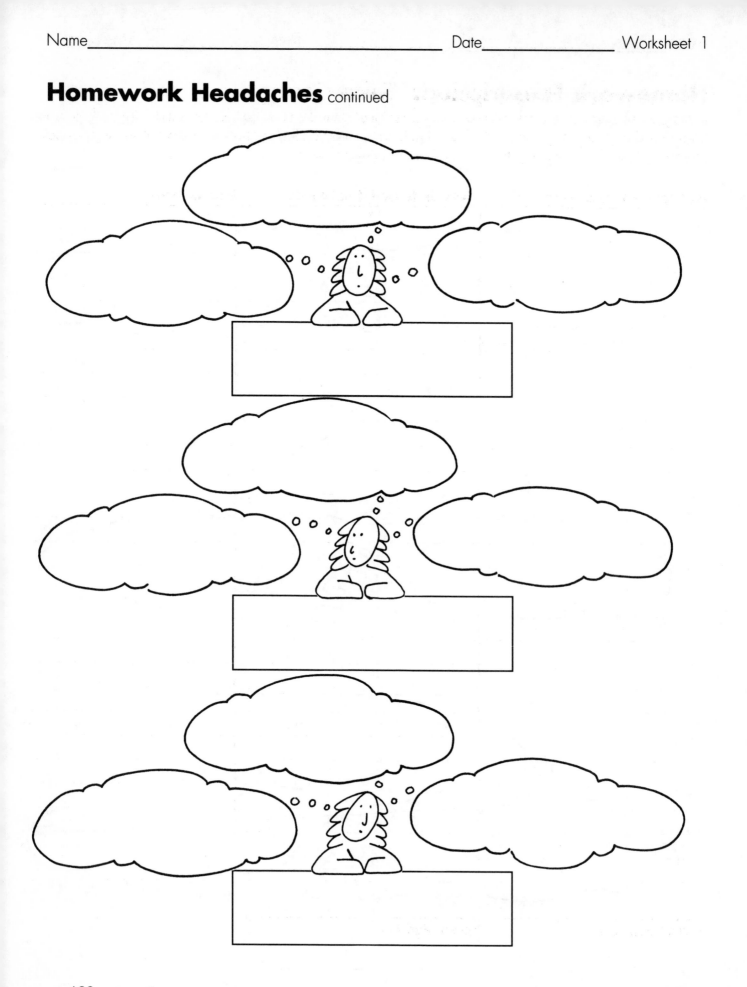

Homework Without Tears for Teachers

Homework Prescription: Take Charge!

In the spaces below, list each homework problem that you identified on Worksheet 1. Then, from your "brainstorm" of possible solutions, list a solution for each that you feel might solve the problem. In the weeks ahead, you will be evaluating the effectiveness of these solutions.

Homework Problem	Here is how I'll solve it:	Evaluation

_____   _____
Student signature   Parent signature

Job Skills Survey

Ask two working people to each complete the Job Skills Survey below.

Name of interview subject_____ **Job title**_____
Description of job duties_____
_____

Check off each statement below that applies to your job.

My job requires that I:

☐ show up on time.
☐ can complete a job without being watched over.
☐ can concentrate.
☐ do my work accurately, without many errors.
☐ know how to get information I need.
☐ plan my work so that it all gets done on time.
☐ know what supplies I need and have them on hand.
☐ know how to plan how long different tasks will take.
☐ accept responsibility for the work I do.
☐ follow directions accurately.
☐ complete work to the best of my ability.
☐ manage time.
☐ manage many projects at once.

Name of interview subject_____ **Job title**_____
Description of job duties_____
_____

Check off each statement below that applies to your job.

My job requires that I:

☐ show up on time.
☐ can complete a job without being watched over.
☐ can concentrate.
☐ do my work accurately, without many errors.
☐ know how to get information I need.
☐ plan my work so that it all gets done on time.
☐ know what supplies I need and have them on hand.
☐ know how to plan how long different tasks will take.
☐ accept responsibility for the work I do.
☐ follow directions accurately.
☐ complete work to the best of my ability.
☐ manage time.
☐ manage many projects at once.

Job Skills—Homework Skills

Part 1: Choose a job that you would like to have, either now or in the future. Write a description of this job. Then, in the spaces below, list seven job skills that would be important to being successful at this job. Choose these seven skills from the list on the Job Skills Survey. Tell specifically why each would be important to the job.

Job Title: _____
Job Description: _____

Important job skills:	**Why is this skill important to the job?**
1 _____	_____
_____	_____
2 _____	_____
_____	_____
3 _____	_____
_____	_____
4 _____	_____
_____	_____
5 _____	_____
_____	_____
6 _____	_____
_____	_____
7 _____	_____
_____	_____

Part 2: What "job skills" did you use to complete this homework assignment. Check off each each box below that describes something you did to finish this assignment.

To complete this homework assignment, I:

- ☐ completed a job without being watched over.
- ☐ concentrated.
- ☐ worked accurately.
- ☐ got the information I needed.
- ☐ planned the work so it got done on time.
- ☐ had the supplies I needed to get the job done.
- ☐ scheduled enough time to finish the assignment.
- ☐ accept the responsibility for my work.
- ☐ followed directions.
- ☐ did the work correctly to the best of my ability.

Study Area Survey

Part 1

I usually do my homework in (name the location):_____
_____
_____

Briefly describe your study area. _____
_____
_____

These are the advantages of this study area: _____
_____
_____
_____
_____

These are the disadvantages of this study area: _____
_____
_____
_____

Part 2

From now on I will do my homework in: _____
_____
_____
_____

This location will be a good study area because: _____
_____
_____
_____
_____

I have agreed on this study area.

_____
Parent signature

_____
Student signature

Homework Survival Kit Checklist

One of the keys to getting homework done is having supplies in one place. A Homework Survival Kit will prevent you from continually being distracted by the need to go searching for supplies, and will free you from last-minute trips to the store for paper, note cards, folders, etc.

These are the items you should have in your Homework Survival Kit:

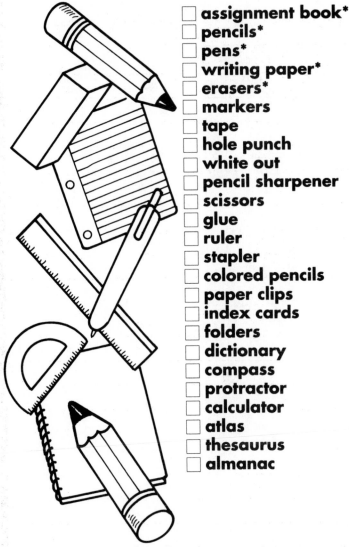

- ☐ **assignment book***
- ☐ **pencils***
- ☐ **pens***
- ☐ **writing paper***
- ☐ **erasers***
- ☐ **markers**
- ☐ **tape**
- ☐ **hole punch**
- ☐ **white out**
- ☐ **pencil sharpener**
- ☐ **scissors**
- ☐ **glue**
- ☐ **ruler**
- ☐ **stapler**
- ☐ **colored pencils**
- ☐ **paper clips**
- ☐ **index cards**
- ☐ **folders**
- ☐ **dictionary**
- ☐ **compass**
- ☐ **protractor**
- ☐ **calculator**
- ☐ **atlas**
- ☐ **thesaurus**
- ☐ **almanac**

*These are the most important supplies you need. Try to obtain these items as soon as possible. Add additional homework supplies as you are able to.

I agree to help my son/daughter put together a Homework Survival Kit.

_____

Parent signature

Daily Schedule

Write down all scheduled activities (music lessons, sports practices, etc.) and reponsibilities (jobs, chores around the house, etc.) for each day of the week so you can clearly see what time is available for homework. Think about your personal time patterns and write in the best time for you to do homework each day. Mark your selected Daily Homework Time for each day in the spaces below.

Monday	Tuesday	Wednesday	Thursday	Friday
8:00	8:00	8:00	8:00	8:00
8:30	8:30	8:30	8:30	8:30
9:00	9:00	9:00	9:00	9:00
9:30	9:30	9:30	9:30	9:30
10:00	10:00	10:00	10:00	10:00
10:30	10:30	10:30	10:30	10:30
11:00	11:00	11:00	11:00	11:00
11:30	11:30	11:30	11:30	11:30
12:00	12:00	12:00	12:00	12:00
12:30	12:30	12:30	12:30	12:30
1:00	1:00	1:00	1:00	1:00
1:30	1:30	1:30	1:30	1:30
2:00	2:00	2:00	2:00	2:00
2:30	2:30	2:30	2:30	2:30
3:00	3:00	3:00	3:00	3:00
3:30	3:30	3:30	3:30	3:30
4:00	4:00	4:00	4:00	4:00
4:30	4:30	4:30	4:30	4:30
5:00	5:00	5:00	5:00	5:00
5:30	5:30	5:30	5:30	5:30
6:00	6:00	6:00	6:00	6:00
6:30	6:30	6:30	6:30	6:30
7:00	7:00	7:00	7:00	7:00
7:30	7:30	7:30	7:30	7:30
8:00	8:00	8:00	8:00	8:00
8:30	8:30	8:30	8:30	8:30
9:00	9:00	9:00	9:00	9:00
9:30	9:30	9:30	9:30	9:30
10:00	10:00	10:00	10:00	10:00

Homework Without Tears for Teachers

© 1989 Lee Canter & Associates Inc.

A.C.E!

Read the acronyms on this page. Each acronym is a positive message about homework.
Create positive messages of your own in the blank spaces. Cut out and use these squares to identify homework
that you are particularly proud of having done on your own.

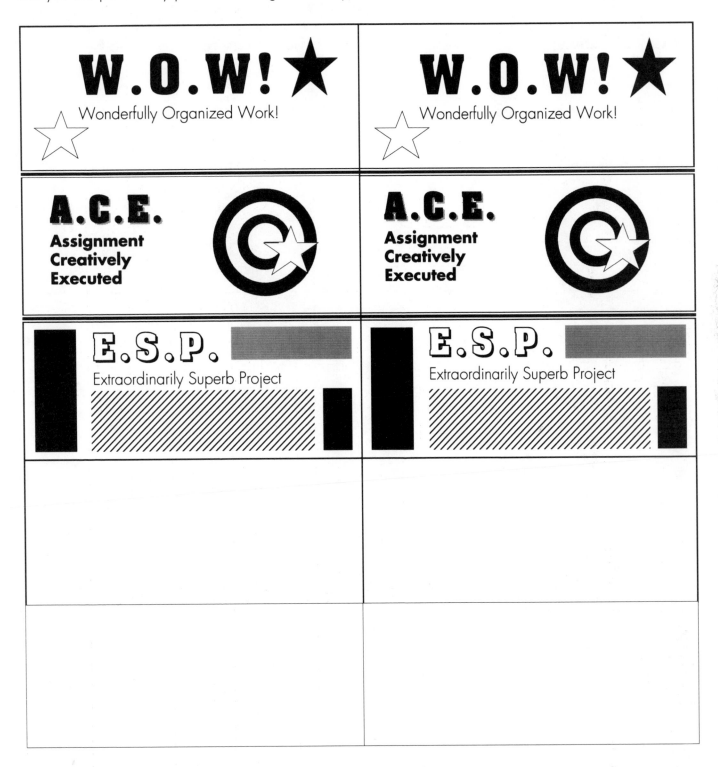

Reward Yourself! You Deserve It!

You don't have to wait for others to tell you you're doing a great job. You can do it yourself! In the spaces below, list study and homework situations for which you might want to give yourself a little reward. Next to each situation, write a reward that might be appropriate. Remember, these rewards must be things that you really can give yourself. Each time you give yourself the reward, check it off.

Study Situation	**This is how I can reward myself.**
Finished 10 math problems	
Read a chapter in social studies	
Wrote note cards on a chapter in science	
Finished a research paper!	

Speedwriting Shortcuts

When you write assignments on an assignment sheet, you have to get a lot of information into a small amount of space. You can make the job easier and faster by learning a few speedwriting shortcuts.

Speedwriting Shortcut #1

Use standard abbreviations when possible.

States, countries, directions, days of the week and months of the year all have familiar abbreviations. Here are examples of several standard abbreviations. Written next to each abbreviation is its definition.

ch.	chapter
e.g.	for example
etc.	and so forth
p.	page
pp.	pages

In the spaces below, write more standard abbreviations and their definitions. (You will find additional abbreviations listed at the back of a dictionary.)

_____

_____

_____

_____

_____

Speedwriting Shortcut #2

Use symbols when possible.

A symbol is a mark or sign that represents something. You can save a lot of space and time on your assignment sheet by using symbols instead of words.

Look at each symbol below. In the space given, write what the symbol represents.

$ _____   & _____

+ _____   = _____

? _____   < _____

> _____   # _____

@ _____   % _____

Speedwriting Shortcut #3
Delete silent letters.

This speedwriting shortcut is effective because it's so easy to use. All you have to do is get into the habit of leaving out vowels as you write words down.

Examples:

bk   (book)
pn   (pen)
rvw   (review)

Keep in mind that if a word contains an important sounded vowel, you may choose to leave it in.

Decode these words.

mth _____	orgniz _____
pn & pncl _____	hmwrk _____
ntbk _____	ppr _____

Now use Speedwriting Shortcut #3 to write a shortened version of each of the following words. Remember to leave out vowels whenever possible.

school _____	book _____
test _____	read _____
lunch _____	ruler _____
computer _____	study _____
library _____	research paper _____

Practice Assignment Sheet

Read the homework assignments written below. Then rewrite each one on the practice assignment sheet. Use speedwriting shortcuts to save time and space, but be sure to include all of the important information. Remember, there is not just *one* correct way to use abbreviations and shortcuts. Use what works best for you.

Math
Do problems 1-24 on page 68.
Show work on even-numbered problems only.
Review formulas in chapter 10.

English
Read chapter 4 in English book.
Do exercises 5 through 9.
Choose biography for book report by Friday.

Social Studies
Review chapter 10.
Answer questions 3, 6, 9, and 14 on page 124.
Watch "Crisis in Asia" on channel 4 tonight.
Final outline for research paper is due on Wednesday.

Spanish
Translate the paragraphs on page 46.
Oral presentation on holidays in Mexico due Monday, April 16.
Remember to bring *Don Quixote* to class tomorrow.

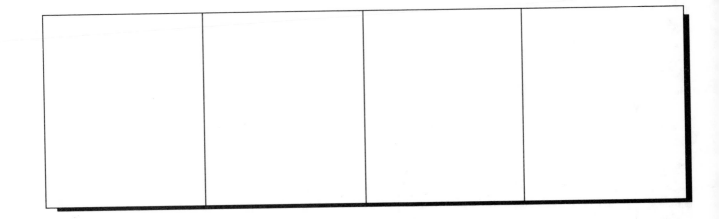

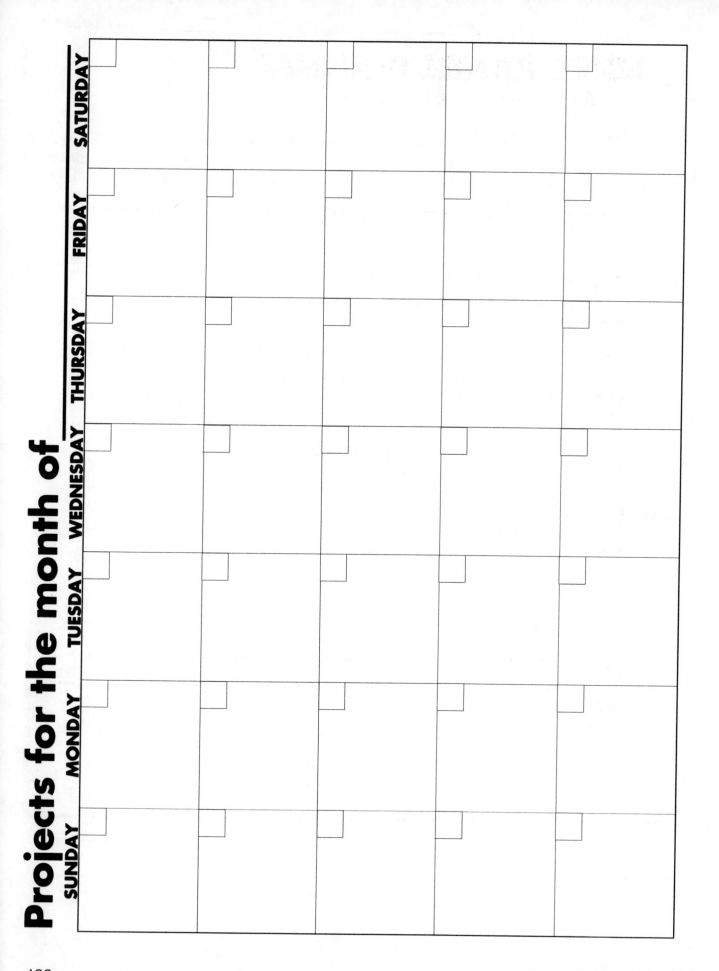

Projects for the month of

| SUNDAY | MONDAY | TUESDAY | WEDNESDAY | THURSDAY | FRIDAY | SATURDAY |

Homework Without Tears for Teachers

LONG-RANGE PLANNER

ASSIGNMENT _____

DUE DATE _____

_____

1 _____ Due Date_____
_____ Parent's Initials_____

2 _____ Due Date_____
_____ Parent's Initials_____

3 _____ Due Date_____
_____ Parent's Initials_____

4 _____ Due Date_____
_____ Parent's Initials_____

5 _____ Due Date_____
_____ Parent's Initials_____

6 _____ Due Date_____
_____ Parent's Initials_____

7 _____ Due Date_____
_____ Parent's Initials_____

Positive Notes for Parents

Run off copies of these notes and keep them handy for use throughout the year.

HOMEWORK NEWS FLASH

Dear _____,

Thought you'd like to know that

_____

is doing a great job on homework

because _____

_____

_____

_____

Signed _____

Date _____

Dear _____

CONGRATULATIONS!

_____
Student's name

did a great job on homework today because

_____

_____

_____

Signed _____

Date _____

Positive Notes for Parents

Run off copies of these notes and keep them handy for use throughout the year.

HOMEWORK PRIVILEGE
PASS ★
_____
Student

HOMEWORK PRIVILEGE
PASS ★
_____
Student

HOMEWORK PRIVILEGE
PASS ★
_____
Student

HOMEWORK PRIVILEGE
PASS ★
_____
Student

HOMEWORK PRIVILEGE
PASS ★
_____
Student

HOMEWORK PRIVILEGE
PASS ★
_____
Student

PARENT RESOURCE SHEETS

When there is a homework-related problem you need help with, contact the parents by phone or in a face-to-face meeting. With the parents discuss the problem the student is having with homework, e.g., forgets to bring assignments home, waits until the last minute to finish assignments, etc.

Note: If a student is having serious problems with homework in your class, it is likely that the problems are also occuring in other classes. Before sending a resource sheet home, it would be a good idea to first discuss the situation with the student's other teachers.

How to use the resource sheets:

Select the appropriate resource sheet and go over each of the steps to make sure the parent understands what is to be done. Then send the sheet home to the parents.

Set a time (in a week or two) to follow up with the parents to determine whether the strategy has been effective or if further action is necessary.

Parent Resource Sheets

Note: You are welcome to translate these pages into any language appropriate for your parents.

For the parent(s) of_____

Homework is an excellent way to teach your child to accept responsibility. To do homework successfully, he or she must learn the importance of starting, sticking with and completing a job. It is also an opportunity to teach your child to do the best work he or she can. Rushing through homework in order to watch TV, talk on the telephone, or go out with friends is common at this age. You need to be clear that doing homework and doing it well is a responsibility. Letting your child rush through an assignment or do sloppy work is teaching that it is all right not to do his or her best work.

Here's what to do when your child doesn't do his or her best work:

1 | State your expectations.

"I have been looking at your homework assignments and I know you can do a better job. You are not to rush through your assignments. I want you to take your time and do the best work you can. Sloppy work with a lot of mistakes is not acceptable."

2 | Use praise for good work.

Simply telling your child what you expect may be enough to inspire better work. If so, your child is doing better work *for you* and you need to be there to recognize it. After you have talked with your child, check the next assignment completed. If the work is better, praise the effort by saying things like, "Great job getting your homework done," or "I like how neat your work is today. Keep up the good work." Praising your child for good work is the best way to encourage continued good efforts.

3 | Institute Mandatory Homework Time.

If your child still rushes through homework, it is probably because the faster it is done the more time he or she will have to spend with friends or watch TV. Mandatory Homework Time takes away these advantages of getting homework done as fast as possible.

Mandatory Homework Time means that a child must use the entire scheduled Daily Homework Time for homework or other academic activities *whether or not homework is completed.* In other words, if two hours are allotted each night (8:00 p.m.—10:00 p.m., for instance), the entire two hours must be spent on homework. If homework is finished, the rest of the time must be spent on other academic work such as reading, or reviewing textbooks or class notes. When students learn that rushing through homework will not be rewarded with more free time, they will learn quickly to slow down and do a better job.

Continued on back

4 | Provide additional incentives.

To encourage your child to continue good work, give a point toward a reward each time homework is completed. For instance, each night he or she does a good job on homework, one point is earned. When five points are earned the child is rewarded with an extra privilege.

5 | If all else fails, contact the teacher.

If after trying the first four steps your child is still not doing his or her best work, contact the teacher. You and the teacher must work together to improve your child's performance.

KEEP THIS IN MIND: You cannot allow your child to be indifferent about homework. If your child learns that it is all right not to do his or her best work, that attitude can be carried outside of school to a job where a boss is much less sympathetic about sloppy work. Now is the time to impress upon your child the importance of doing the best work he or she is capable of.

For the parent(s) of_____

When your child would rather battle with you every night rather than do homework, it is time to set firm limits. Your child may openly refuse to do homework or lie to you or to the teacher about why it hasn't been done. To solve this problem, you must make it clear to your child that choosing not to do homework is choosing not to enjoy certain privileges.

Here's what to do when your child refuses to do homework assignments:

1 State clearly how you expect homework to be completed.

Tell your child, "I expect you to do all of your homework every night. Under no circumstances will I tolerate your refusing to do your homework assignments."

2 Back up your words with actions.

When your child is engaged in a power struggle with you and refuses to do homework, you must make it clear that his or her behavior will result in a loss of privileges. Tell your child: "You can choose either to do your homework or to not have privileges. If you choose not to do your homework, then, until you have finished your assignments, you will lose these privileges: You will not leave this house. You will not watch TV. You will not be allowed to listen to music or use the telephone. You will sit here until all of your homework is done. The choice is yours." Then, stick with your demands. It may take your child several days of sitting idly in his or her study area to realize that you mean business.

3 Praise your child when homework is done.

Praise your child each time he or she does homework. "I really like the way you've been getting your homework done. That's what I expect from you."

4 Use a Homework Contract to provide additional incentives.

A Homework Contract is an effective motivator for young people of any age. It is an especially valuable tool because it encourages your child to accept responsibility for an agreement between you that states: "When you do your homework, you will earn a reward." For example: "Each day that you bring home your homework and complete it during Daily Homework Time, you will earn one point. When you have earned 10 points, you may earn a special privilege."

Continued on back

5 **If all else fails, contact the teacher.**

If problems persist, contact the teacher and request that additional discipline be provided at school for homework assignments not completed. Your child will quickly learn that the school is backing up your efforts.

KEEP THIS IN MIND: Students must learn that homework is not a battleground. There can be no power struggle over homework. It must be done. Your child must learn that conflict on this issue will not be tolerated.

For the parent(s) of_____

From time to time your child may forget to bring home books or homework assignments. But when he or she continually fails to bring home assigned homework, you must take action.

Here's what to do when your child fails to bring assignments home:

1 State clearly that you expect all homework assignments to be brought home.

Tell your child, "I expect you to bring home all your assigned work and all the books you need to complete your assignments. If you finish your homework during free time at school, I expect you to bring it home so that I can see it."

2 Work with your child's teachers to make sure that you know what homework has been assigned.

Students should be writing all homework assignments down on a weekly assignment sheet. Ask your child's teachers to check and sign the assignment sheet at the end of each class. When your child completes the assignments, you sign the sheet and have your child return it to the teacher.

3 Provide praise and support when all homework assignments are brought home.

Make sure that your child knows that you appreciate it every time he or she brings home all homework assignments. "It's great to see that you remembered to bring home all of your homework. I knew you could do it."

4 Institute Mandatory Homework Time.

If your child still fails to bring home assignments, he or she may be avoiding homework in favor of spending time with friends or watching TV. Mandatory Homework Time eliminates the advantages of forgetting homework. Mandatory Homework Time means that your child must use the entire scheduled Daily Homework Time for homework or other academic activities whether homework is brought home or not. In other words, if two hours are allotted each night for homework, the entire time must be spent on homework. If homework is not brought home, the entire time must be spend on other academic work such as reading, or reviewing textbooks or class notes. When students learn that their irresponsible approach to homework will not be rewarded with more free time, they will learn quickly to remember to bring home their assignments.

Continued on back

5 | Use a Homework Contract to provide additional incentives.

A Homework Contract is an effective motivator for students of any age. It is an especially valuable tool because it encourages your child to accept responsibility for an agreement between you that states, "When you do your homework, you will earn a reward." For example: "Each day that you bring home your homework and complete it during Daily Homework Time, you will earn one point. When you have earned ten points, you may earn a special privilege."

6 | If all else fails, work with teachers to follow through at school for homework not completed.

If your child continues to forget homework, discuss with teachers involved the possibility of imposing loss of privileges at school. Loss of lunch time, or assigning after-school detention, lets your child know that you and the school are working together to ensure that he or she behaves responsibly.

KEEP THIS IN MIND: Your child must learn to bring home and complete all homework assignments. Accept no excuses.

For the parent(s) of _____

If your child puts off starting long-range assignments until just before they are due, it can put stress on the entire family. Typically, this child waits until the last minute, and then goes into a frenzy, demanding your immediate help. To solve this problem, you must take steps to teach your child about long-range planning.

Here's what to do when your child waits until the last minute to finish assignments:

1 Make it clear that you expect long-range projects to be planned and completed responsibly.

Sit down with your child and say that you will not tolerate putting off projects until just before they are due. "I expect you to plan your project responsibly. This waiting until the last minute must stop."

2 Ask the teacher for a Long-Range Planner.

Often students have trouble with big projects because they have never learned how to organize such assignments. The key is to get into the habit of breaking the big project down into smaller parts, each with its own deadline. Ask your child's teacher to give your child a Long-Range Planner. By using the Long-Range Planner, your child will learn how to break down a large project into small, easily completed tasks and how to distribute the assignments over the period of time given for the project. Insist that your child tell you about each long-range assignment and then help him or her use the planner to decide when each step of the project is to be completed.

3 Provide praise and support as each step is completed.

Each time your child completes a step of a long-range project, let him or her know how pleased you are: "I think that it's terrific that you've already chosen the topic of your research report. Keep up the good work!"

4 Provide additional motivators when appropriate.

If your child needs additional motivation to complete a long-range project on time, institute a system that allows him or her to earn a point toward a reward or privilege each time a step is completed according to the schedule.

Continued on back

5 | Back up your words with action.

If the first four steps fail to motivate your child to do long-range planning, it's time to impose restrictions. If the child fails to (for example) read a book selected for a book report by the agreed-upon date, take away a privilege (use of the telephone, going to the mall, watching TV) until the book is read. Unless you set limits, your child is not going to believe that you mean business.

KEEP THIS IN MIND: Your child must learn to budget the time allocated for long-range projects. It is a skill that must be developed if your child is to be capable of taking on larger tasks as he or she grows up.

CREATIVE HOMEWORK MODEL WORKSHEETS

Pages 149-153 of the Appendix contain the reproducible worksheets for the Creative Homework Models presented in Chapter 9. Make one copy of each worksheet per student prior to giving the lesson.

Creative Homework Model Worksheets:

Name_____ Date_____

Role Play

Imagine that you _____

_____

Write a journal page _____

_____

Name_____ Date_____

Pros and Cons

Inside the spaces below list two reasons **for** and two reasons **against** _____
_____

Which argument do you favor? Explain your reasons.

_____
_____
_____
_____

Name_____ Date_____

Looking Into the Library

Using the

- ☐ dictionary
- ☐ encyclopedia
- ☐ thesaurus
- ☐ atlas
- ☐ almanac
- ☐ *Guiness Book of World Records*

_____

_____

_____

_____

_____

_____

_____

_____

_____

_____

_____

_____

_____

_____

_____

_____

_____

_____

_____

_____

_____

Name_____ Date_____

Etcetera, Etcetera, Etcetera!

List _____

_____

Circle your favorite. In the space below, explain why it is your favorite.

_____

_____

_____

Name_____ Date_____

Triple-Decker Homework

Do_____ problems from the top, the middle and the bottom of page _____
of your _____ book.

Write and solve the problems in the spaces below.

RECOMMENDED READING

For readers desiring more information about homework, the following works are recommended for the subject areas listed below.

ACADEMIC ACHIEVEMENT

Fredrick, W.C., & Walberg, H.J. (1980). Learning as a function of time. *Journal of Educational Research, 73,* 183-204.

Keith, T. (1986). *Homework.* West Lafayette, IN.: Kappa Delta Pi.

Lavin, D.E. (1965). *The prediction of academic performance.* New York: Russell Sage Foundation.

EFFECTIVENESS FOR HIGH AND LOW ACHIEVERS

Keith, T.Z. (1982). Time spent on homework and high school grades: A large-sample path analysis. *Journal of Educational Psychology, 74,* 248-253.

Stanley, op. cit.

EFFECTIVENESS AT THE HIGH SCHOOL LEVEL

Coleman, J.S., Hoffer, T., & Kilgore, S. (1981). *Public and private schools.* Washington, D.C.: U.S. Department of Education.

Foyle, H.C. (1984). The effects of preparation and practice homework on student achievement in tenth-grade American history. (Doctoral dissertation, Kansas State University, 1984). *Dissertation Abstracts International.*

Keith, T.Z. (1982). op. cit.

Keith, T.Z., & Page, E.B. (1985). Homework works at school: National evidence for policy changes. *School Psychology Review, 14.*

QUALITY VERSUS QUANTITY

Leonard, M.H. (1965). An experimental study of homework at the intermediate-grade level. *Dissertation Abstracts International, 26,* 3782.